D1558411

Strategy for U.S. Industrial Competitiveness

**A Statement by the Research and
Policy Committee of the Committee
for Economic Development**

April 1984

CED

Library of Congress Cataloging in Publication Data

Committee for Economic Development. Subcommittee
  on Industrial Strategy and Trade.
  Strategy for U.S. industrial competitiveness.

  Includes bibliographical references.
  1. Industry and state—United States.   2. United
States—Commercial policy.   I. Committee for Economic
Development.   Research and Policy Committee.   II. Title.
III. Title: Strategy for US industrial competitiveness.
HD3616.U47C535   1984   338.973   84-7023
ISBN   0-87186-778-8
ISBN   0-87186-078-3 (pbk.)

First printing in bound-book form: July 1984
Paperback: $9.50
Library binding: $11.50
Printed in the United States of America
Design: Stead Young & Rowe Inc

COMMITTEE FOR ECONOMIC DEVELOPMENT
477 Madison Avenue, New York, N.Y. 10022
1700 K Street N.W., Washington, D.C. 20006

CONTENTS

iv

Strategy for
U.S. Industrial
Competitiveness

RESPONSIBILITY FOR CED STATEMENTS ON NATIONAL POLICY

The Committee for Economic Development is an independent research and educational organization of two hundred business executives and educators. CED is nonprofit, nonpartisan, and nonpolitical. Its purpose is to propose policies that will help to bring about steady economic growth at high employment and reasonably stable prices, increase productivity and living standards, provide greater and more equal opportunity for every citizen, and improve the quality of life for all. A more complete description of CED appears on page 144.

All CED policy recommendations must have the approval of trustees on the Research and Policy Committee. This committee is directed under the bylaws to "initiate studies into the principles of business policy and of public policy which will foster the full contribution by industry and commerce to the attainment and maintenance" of the objectives stated above. The bylaws emphasize that "all research is to be thoroughly objective in character, and the approach in each instance is to be from the standpoint of the general welfare and not from that of any special political or economic group." The committee is aided by a Research Advisory Board of leading social scientists and by a small permanent professional staff.

The Research and Policy Committee does not attempt to pass judgment on any pending specific legislative proposals; its purpose is to urge careful consideration of the objectives set forth in this statement and of the best means of accomplishing those objectives.

Each statement is preceded by extensive discussions, meetings, and exchange of memoranda. The research is undertaken by a subcommittee, assisted by advisors chosen for their competence in the field under study. The members and advisors of the subcommittee that prepared this statement are listed on pages viii and ix.

The full Research and Policy Committee participates in the drafting of recommendations. Likewise, the trustees on the drafting subcommittee vote to approve or disapprove a policy statement, and they share with the Research and Policy Committee the privilege of submitting individual comments for publication, as noted on pages 134 through 142 of this statement.

Except for the members of the Research and Policy Committee and the responsible subcommittee, the recommendations presented herein are not necessarily endorsed by other trustees or by the advisors, contributors, staff members, or others associated with CED.

RESEARCH AND POLICY COMMITTEE

ADVISORS

THOMAS R. ATKINSON
Vice President
General Motors Overseas Corporation

GARRY D. BREWER
Professor of Political Science
Yale University

RICHARD N. COOPER
Maurits C. Boas Professor of International Economics
Harvard University

WILLIAM DIEBOLD, JR.
Senior Research Fellow
Council on Foreign Relations

GEORGE C. EADS
School of Public Affairs
The University of Maryland

GEORGE C. LODGE
Professor
Harvard Business School

EDWIN R. MacKETHAN
Director, Business Environment, Evaluation, Corporate
  Strategy and Analysis Staff
Ford Motor Company

PETER B. MULLONEY
Vice President and Assistant to the Chairman
United States Steel Corporation

FRANK W. SCHIFF
Vice President and Chief Economist
Committee for Economic Development

JUDITH N. SHAPIRO
Manager, Government Issues Development
General Electric Company

RICHARD WOOL
Senior Advisor, Public Affairs
Pfizer Inc.

PROJECT CO-DIRECTORS

ISAIAH FRANK
William L. Clayton Professor of International Economics
The Johns Hopkins University

KENNETH McLENNAN
Vice President and Director of Industrial Studies
Committee for Economic Development

PROJECT STAFF

LORRAINE M. BROOKER
Economic Research Associate

PEGGY MORRISSETTE
Deputy Director, Governmental Affairs, and Deputy
  Secretary, Research and Policy Committee

NATHANIEL M. SEMPLE
Vice President, Director of Governmental Affairs, and
  Secretary, Research and Policy Committee

PROJECT EDITOR

CLAUDIA P. FEUREY
Vice President and Director of Information

Dedicated to

J. Paul Lyet

1917-1984

who brought uncommon wisdom,
energy, and judgment to his
leadership of this project

Purpose Of This Statement

A primary mission of the Committee for Economic Development is to identify, study, and make recommendations on some of the key long-term problems facing the nation and the economy. For a number of years now, CED's trustees have become increasingly concerned with declining U.S. competitiveness in world markets, with sluggish domestic productivity, and with rising competition from developed and developing countries alike.

In effect, what we have been witnessing during the past years is not just an abstract erosion in economic preeminence, but a real and serious threat to this nation's ability to compete, to maintain let alone raise its citizens' standard of living, and ultimately, to the nation's national security.

CED's response to these very serious threats has been to launch a series of studies aimed at improving various aspects of U.S. competitiveness. In recent years, CED has issued major statements on technology policy, productivity, and economic growth and inflation which have recommended public and private policies to reinvigorate the American economy.

In this statement, we have drawn particularly from the work of two recent CED projects, *Stimulating Technological Progress* (1980) and *Productivity Policy: Key to the Nation's Economic Future* (1983).

CED's research and policy agenda covers a number of other issues that are crucial for a vigorous and growing economy. These include adequate public education and ways in which business can help improve the public schools, techniques for stimulating state economic progress, a new look at the U.S. tax system, and policies for reducing federal budget deficits.

THE CED APPROACH TO INDUSTRIAL STRATEGY

In this report, CED Trustees have addressed directly some of the real issues we feel are basic to rebuilding competitiveness — policies to stimulate overall economic growth, regulatory and antitrust reforms, government assistance to industries and workers, and how to compete with the fast-paced, fast-changing international economy.

In formulating their recommendations, the Trustees of the subcommittee that prepared this report were keenly aware of the many proposals for "industrial policies" that are currently under discussion — ranging from removal of most or all government restraints or incentives to a government-structured and directed system of guided economic growth.

After studying the problems facing the nation and the proposed options, we have specifically rejected a course of action that would increase government involvement in the economy or that would artificially steer the economy in some predetermined direction. Rather we call for a set of market-oriented policies that we believe will help free the competitive energies of the American economy and which we believe offer the best hope of allowing the economy to grow and flourish.

ACKNOWLEDGEMENTS

It is with deep regret that I note the passing of J. Paul Lyet, vice chairman of the CED Board of Trustees, under whose inspired leadership this policy statement was completed. Paul, who was former chairman of Sperry Corporation and chairman of the President's Export Council, brought a depth of knowledge and experience to this project and an extraordinary ability to forge consensus on a complex set of issues. With heartfelt gratitude, we dedicate this report to him.

I would like to thank the especially able group of CED Trustees and advisors who served on the CED subcommittee that prepared this report. A list of their names appears on pages viii and ix.

I also wish to thank the co-project directors Isaiah Frank, William L. Clayton Professor of International Economics at The Johns Hopkins University School of Advanced International Studies, and Kenneth McLennan, CED Vice President and Director of Industrial Studies for the insight, scholarship, and dedication they brought to this project. Thanks are also due to George C. Eads for his contribution to the section on regulation and antitrust.

And finally, we are deeply indebted to The Andrew W. Mellon Foundation for both its generosity and its concern for the future of the American economy which helped make this project possible. We also wish to thank The American Express Company for their contribution to the project's focus on international trade.

William F. May
Chairman
Research and Policy Committee

Chapter 1

Introduction and Summary of Recommendations

The era of unquestioned U.S. dominance in the world economy is clearly over, and has been for some time. The combined forces of lagging U.S. productivity performance and the rising competitiveness of other countries leave us with no choice but to adopt policies to strengthen our competitive position if we wish to increase the real economic well being of the American people and maintain our position as a leading economic power in the world.

Neither further government involvement in the economy nor new policies or institutions designed to steer the economy in some predetermined direction will increase U.S. competitiveness. Rather, the most effective, and perhaps the only successful, path to increased U.S. international competitiveness is through:

- placing significantly more reliance on free market forces, and

- reforming necessary government interventions to provide an economic environment which stimulates innovation in the private sector and helps resources adapt to changing competition.

Increased interference with the market economy will weaken it further, harming business, workers, and consumers alike.

Structural economic change, through technological advances, shifts in consumer preferences and the growing importance of a global economy, is a continuous process. Over time, the relative importance of some industrial sectors in the economy declines, but this does not mean that the U.S. industrial base will be eroded or that our manufacturing capability will inevitably decline.

As shown in Figure 1, the contribution of manufacturing to the output of the economy has remained relatively stable over the past two decades, even as service-producing industries have become slightly more important. Continuous economic change, however, has redistributed the labor force among major industrial sectors. Even though in absolute terms manufacturing employment grew during the past two decades, its relative share of non-agricultural employment declined chiefly because of the surge in service employment. This decline in the manufacturing sector's share of total employment was most pronounced during the 1960s, not the 1970s (Figure 2).

Since 1980 we have experienced the most severe setback in economic activity in the post-World War II period. Figure 3 shows that the service-producing sectors have continued to grow in relative importance as a source of both output and employment. On the other hand, goods-producing industries — and especially manufacturing industries which are very sensitive to changes in economic activity — lost both employment and share of the labor force after 1980. A strong recovery from the recent recession has rapidly expanded employment in the goods-producing industries, and government projections predict that manufacturing employment will continue to expand through 1990.* It is not yet clear, however, whether this recession has produced any *major* permanent change in the structure of the economy. What is certain is that significant changes in the employment distribution of industries *within* manufacturing and nonmanufacturing sectors will continue throughout the remainder of this decade, and may prove to be more rapid than in the past.

Judged by total output comparisons, the U.S. economy is not "deindustrializing," but important structural changes have occurred *within* sectors of the economy and some industries and firms have lost competitiveness. Neither a strong economic recovery nor more favorable exchange rates achieved through improved general economic policies will fully restore the former competitive position of many of these firms. At the same time, some industries in both the manufacturing and nonmanufacturing sectors have improved their competitive position and are now more important sources of output and employment growth.

Of course, it makes no economic sense for U.S. companies to try to be leading competitors in *every* industry. But since productivity growth rates in some U.S. industries have been consistently lower than comparable rates of

---

*See memorandum by HENRY B. SCHACHT, page 134.

FIGURE 1

Long-Term Structural Change in Distribution
of Nonagricultural Output

- Manufacturing contribution to GNP remained the same, despite cyclical variation.

- Relative contribution of other goods-producing sectors declined slightly.

- Relative contribution of all service-producing sectors increased slightly except government, which declined substantially.

Industry	1960	1970	1980	Change 1960-1970	Change 1970-1980
Mining	1.8	1.7	1.5	−0.1	−0.2
Construction	6.3	4.9	3.7	−1.4	−1.2
Manufacturing	23.3	24.1	23.7	+0.8	−0.4
Transportation and public utilities	7.8	8.7.	9.7	+0.9	+1.0
Wholesale and retail trade	15.9	16.2	16.4	+0.3	+0.2
Finance, insurance and real estate	13.9	14.4	16.0	+0.5	+1.6
Services	11.3	11.7	12.4	+0.4	+0.7
Government	14.6	14.1	11.9	−0.5	−2.2

Relative Contribution
Percent of Gross National Product by Industry Division
(1960, 1970, 1980)

SOURCE: Calculations for figure 1 are based on data in *Employment and Earnings* 31, no. 1 (Washington, D.C.: U.S. Department of Labor, Bureau of Labor Statistics, January 1984), p. 85; and *Economic Report of the President* (Washington, D.C.: U.S. Government Printing Office, 1984), p. 233.

4

FIGURE 2

Long-Term Structural Change in Distribution of Nonagricultural Employment

- In both the 1960s and 1970s, all sectors experienced an average annual increase in employment, except mining, which declined in the 1960s.

- As a proportion of the labor force, all goods-producing sectors declined in the 1960s and 1970s, except mining, which increased its share slightly in the 1970s.

- For manufacturing, the decline in the share of the labor force was larger in the 1960s than in the 1970s.

- All service-producing sectors increased their share of the labor force in both the 1960s and 1970s.

Change and Distribution of Employment by Industry Division (1960-1980)				
	1960-1970		1970-1980	
Industry	Average Annual Percent Change in Employment	Proportion of Labor Force (Percentage point change)	Average Annual Percent Change in Employment	Proportion of Labor Force (Percentage point change)
Mining	−1.33	−0.4	5.12	0.2
Construction	2.06	−0.3	1.93	−0.3
Manufacturing	1.43	−3.6	0.46	−0.7
Transportation and public utilities	1.20	−1.0	1.31	1.0
Wholesale and retail trade	2.81	0.2	3.04	1.3
Finance, insurance and real estate	3.32	0.1	3.53	0.6
Services	4.58	2.7	4.47	3.5
Government	4.15	2.3	2.60	0.3

SOURCE: Calculations for figure 2 are based on data in *Employment and Earnings* 31, no. 1 (Washington, D.C.: U.S. Department of Labor, Bureau of Labor Statistics, January 1984), p. 85; and *Economic Report of the President* (Washington, D.C.: U.S. Government Printing Office, 1984), p. 233.

FIGURE 3

Short-Term Changes in Nonagricultural Contribution to GNP and in Employment During 1980-1983 Recessionary Period

- For goods-producing sectors:
  - The contribution to GNP fell during this severe recessionary period.
  - Average annual change in employment was negative as was their share of the labor force.
- For service-producing sectors:
  - The contribution to GNP increased for all sectors except transportation and public utilities.
  - Average annual change in employment was positive for all sectors except transportation and public utilities.
  - Share of the labor force increased for all sectors except transportation and public utilities and government, whose shares declined.

Relative Change in Output and Employment by Industry Division (1980-1983)			
Industry	Contribution to GNP (percent change)*	Annual Average Change in Employment	Change in Proportion of Labor Force
Mining	0	−0.15	0
Construction	−0.5	−2.37	−0.4
Manufacturing	−1.1	−2.05	−1.6
Transportation and public utilities	−0.3	−1.01	−0.2
Wholesale and retail trade	+0.3	+0.24	+0.3
Finance, insurance, and real estate	+0.8	+1.40	+0.3
Services	+1.3	+2.42	+2.1
Government	0	−0.77	−0.5

*Figures in this column represent the change for the 1980-1982 period. GNP data by industry are not available for 1983.

SOURCE: Calculations for figure 3 are based on data in *Employment and Earnings* 31, no. 1 (Washington, D.C.: U.S. Department of Labor, Bureau of Labor Statistics, January 1984), p. 85; and *Economic Report of the President* (Washington, D.C.: U.S. Government Printing Office, 1984), p. 233.

growth in other nations for two decades, the *level* of productivity in one U.S. manufacturing industry after another has been matched and in some cases surpassed by our major competitors. This has been a significant source of the serious and growing loss of competitiveness in some sectors of the U.S. economy.[1] It is difficult to determine the competitive position of industries in the nonmanufacturing sector, but persistent low productivity growth in most of these industries should be a warning that many nonmanufacturing industries are also likely to face increasing competition from foreign rivals.

Our recent history of high rates of inflation, poor productivity, prolonged exchange rate misalignment, and high levels of unemployment are all related to loss of competitiveness and are, of course, causes for very serious concern. During the strong domestic economic recovery of 1983-1984, we have made significant progress in reversing some of these trends, but many of the structural problems underlying our deteriorating competitiveness have not yet been solved. For many sectors of the U.S. economy, the need to revitalize competitiveness has reached the stage of urgency.

The sharply increased price of energy since 1973, the shifting consumer appetite for smaller and imported cars, rising real interest rates, the changing comparative advantage of Japanese, German, and U.S. firms — these and many other developments were of a scope and speed that were simply not foreseen in our economy. While some of these changes were largely beyond the control of both private-sector and government policies, many sources of the current U.S. competitiveness problem can be traced to past and present public policies. U.S. economic policy has long favored consumption over saving and investment, with the result that the investment in future economic growth has been inhibited. Compared to our major industrial competitors the United States has consistently had lower rates of private saving and investment, and in real terms there was little net increase in investment in U.S. manufacturing plant and equipment during 1973-1979. This has contributed importantly to the loss of competitiveness in some U.S. industries.

There has also been a strong current consumption bias in public expenditures. During the 1960s, government transfer payments and grants-in-

---

1. See *Productivity Policy: Key to the Nation's Economic Future* (New York: CED, 1983). Competitiveness will be improved only if productivity growth is *consistently* higher than in the past. Short-term improvements during the early stage of an economic recovery are not sufficient for restoring competitiveness. During the first year of the recovery from the 1981-1982 recession, manufacturing productivity growth was somewhat higher than during recoveries from most previous recessions. But for the private business sector as a whole the improvement was less than the improvement for all recessions since World War II.

aid increased at about 8 percent a year in real terms. This average annual rate of growth in social transfers continued into the 1970s despite a significant decline in productivity growth and a slowing of real economic growth to a little over 3 percent a year. In addition, the growth of the public sector has had the effect of "crowding out" some private sector investment, and government interferences with the price system in some major areas of the economy have resulted in a misallocation of resources without any net social benefit.

To bolster the performance of *all* sectors of the economy, the challenge now is developing concrete, constructive public policies to enable the economy to adapt better to emerging trends with less delay, fewer inefficiencies, and less contradictory actions. Future policies should focus on how to provide individuals with the skills to be flexible in labor markets of the future and how to motivate investors and managers to shift labor and capital resources smoothly toward expanding markets and away from less competitive ones. In short, this nation needs a strategy toward all industries that avoids protecting the status quo and, instead, facilitates adjustment so that the nation can capture the advantages of structural change. With appropriate public and private policy changes, the United States and its trading partners will be in a better position to realize the long-run benefits of expanding international trade in an increasingly interdependent world.

CED's VIEW OF A COMPETITIVE STRATEGY

Governments in all developed economies try to raise industrial output, employment, and productivity. In some countries, these policies are relatively explicit. Some have a stated coordinated strategy of long-term government planning, designating which industries and regions will be assisted. For most countries, however, industrial policies are not comprehensive; they consist of a combination of separate economic development policies, investment incentives, and protection of specific industries from foreign competition.

Recently, there have been calls from a variety of groups with differing political persuasions for the United States to adopt an "industrial policy."* Most of these proposals recommend increased government intervention in markets to affect the pace of economic change and provide preferential government assistance to specific industries and groups of workers.[2]

2. For a review of the major industrial policies, see William F. Baumol and Kenneth McLennan, eds., *Stimulating U.S. Productivity Growth* (New York: Oxford University Press, forthcoming 1984), Chapter 8.

*See memorandum by JOHN DIEBOLD, page 134.

Some industrial policy proposals advocate the establishment of new institutions that would have authority to divert government expenditures and private pension fund assets, and provide preferential loans and tax incentives to assist specific industries and firms. The overall direction of the strategy would be determined to an important extent by a tripartite Industrial Development Board, consisting of representatives of labor, business, and government. Some proponents claim that Industrial Development Board decisions would be only advisory, but at the same time, the board would be responsible for determining the key sectors and regions of the economy that deserve assistance. Management of the targeted assistance program would be in the hands of a new institution, similar in concept to the Japan Development Bank or a reconstituted Reconstruction Finance Corporation. This new independent financial institution would include tripartite representation and would carry out the policies emanating from the Industrial Development Board. Some supporters of this form of market intervention envisage an extensive network of industry and regional boards similar to the approach adopted by the United Kingdom during the 1970s. These boards would have significant power in the allocation of government assistance to specific industries and companies. *This Committee strongly opposes such a strategy for improving U.S. competitiveness.*

Whenever interested parties participate directly and collectively in public policy decisions affecting economic change, there is a strong tendency toward agreement on policies that favor the status quo and impede economic change. And it is likely that those with new ideas will be underrepresented in such collective decision making. The goal of improving U.S. competitiveness thus becomes more difficult to achieve because resources tend to be retained in those economic activities and in firms and industries in which productivity growth is lowest. There is no evidence that a tripartite group of individuals representing diverse interests will be more successful than the market system in identifying the industries and companies which are crucial to the future success of the economy. In fact, U.S. experience has shown that targeted governmental assistance has typically been based on political expediency rather than economic potential.

In sharp contrast with increased government targeting to sectors and regions, *CED emphasizes more reliance on the market system for identifying promising industries and permitting economic activity to decline where firms have lost their basic comparative advantage.* The market system's signals indicate the direction of the forthcoming change while relative price changes provide a strong incentive for management and labor to adjust to industrial, occupational, and geographic changes. If the government resists pressure to intervene in these markets, the market system will in most cases provide gradual structural change.[3]

Over the years, CED has stressed consistently the importance of relying on relative market prices as much as possible for reallocating resources. If the market system is to guide resource allocation, public policies affecting industry should be as neutral as possible and should avoid favoring specific sectors of the economy.

A COMPETITIVE MARKET ECONOMY: COMPONENTS OF CED'S APPROACH

For society to benefit most from continuous structural change in product and labor markets, government must adopt a policy strategy which enables capital and labor resources to move to their most efficient use. CED believes that a competitive market economy is the essential foundation of such a strategy because experience in most industrial nations has shown that "it is normally the best mechanism to marshal responses to social, economic and technological changes, flexibly, constructively and without excessive cost."[4]

Under CED's market-based strategy the prime responsibility for improving competitiveness rests with the private sector — with both managers and their employees. The market system rewards firms that innovate, anticipate changes in demand, and restructure their resources to meet or overtake foreign competition, and it penalizes those that fail to adopt new productive techniques, improve quality, reduce unit costs of production, pursue new markets, or take account of the long-term implications of managerial decisions. Management and labor bear the major responsibility for increasing the speed with which capital and labor resources are reallocated to their most efficient use. In a market-based strategy, compensation inflexibility,

---

3. See George C. Eads, "The Political Experience in Allocating Investment: Lessons from the United States and Elsewhere," in *Toward a New U.S. Industrial Policy?*, eds., Michael L. Wachter and Susan M. Wachter (Philadelphia: University of Pennsylvania Press, 1981), pp. 453-482. For an empirical estimate of the contribution to productivity growth through resource reallocation by the market system, see Frank Gollop, "Evidence for a Sector-Biased or Sector-Neutral Industrial Strategy: Analysis of the Productivity Slowdown," in *Stimulating U.S. Productivity Growth*, eds., Baumol and McLennan.

---

4. Organization for Economic Cooperation and Development Council at Ministerial Level, Positive Adjustment Policies: Managing Structural Change (Paris: Organization for Economic Cooperation and Development, 1982), p. 2.

10

barriers to labor mobility, and hiding behind a wall of protectionism when competitiveness is lost are all detrimental to society, and eventually to those adversely affected by economic change.[5]

Although competitive markets are crucial to the efficient reallocation of resources, they do not always work perfectly. Government policies can improve market performance by reducing restrictions, such as unnecessary market regulations, and by minimizing distortions when government action is required or when society feels the operation of the market is likely to produce some undesirable social result.

In addition, government intervention to improve the operation of markets can be legitimate when markets fail. However, such intervention should be undertaken only if the result of the government action (including the cost) is likely to be superior to the outcome of an imperfectly functioning market.[6]

Public policies should not attempt to halt or modify the pace of structural change. On the contrary, policies should be as neutral as possible in their effect on the allocation of resources. Similarly, when interventions are necessary to assist those hurt by change, the policy instruments should not attempt to preserve the status quo. Public and private policies should be designed to encourage labor and capital resources to adapt so that the benefits of change can be widely distributed throughout society.

In our view, there are three main areas of government policy change that can contribute the most to U.S. industrial competitiveness.* **

- *Overall economic policies need to create a climate for sustained non-inflationary growth and productivity improvement.*

  — Monetary and fiscal policies that control inflation and provide a significant reduction in federal budget deficits are essential. No expenditure programs, including entitlements and national defense, should be automatically excluded from potential reductions. Tax increases can also be used to reduce deficits but any such increase should be designed to avoid inhibiting saving and investment in new plant and equipment.

---

5. For a more detailed review of actions management and labor can take to improve competitiveness, see "What Management and Labor Can Do" in the policy statement *Productivity Policy: Key to the Nation's Economic Future*, Chapter 6.

6. For a complete discussion of the conditions under which markets do not work perfectly and the criteria for selecting the form of government intervention, see the policy statement *Redefining Government's Role in the Market System* (New York: CED, 1979), Chapter 6.

---

*See memorandum by HENRY B. SCHACHT, page 135.

**See memorandum by ELMER B. STAATS, page 136.

— Fiscal and monetary policies need to be balanced appropriately, because a policy imbalance can directly harm the competitiveness of U.S. goods and services in international markets through its influence on real interest rates and exchange rates.

— Tax and expenditure policies should be designed to stimulate growth and competition without distorting the efficient allocation of resources.

- *Unnecessary governmental barriers to efficient market operation need to be reduced.*

— When private markets fail or produce socially undesirable results, government intervention can be justified, but only to the extent that such intervention does not produce a result worse than the initial market failure.

- *Domestic and international policies need to facilitate adjustment to change in markets and help the nation reap the maximum benefits of trade.*

— Business should be encouraged to shift the allocation of resources in response to changes in international markets so that society will benefit fully from increased trade. But at the same time, U.S. policy must be prepared to react when other countries provide domestic industries with protection from international competition in order to target certain of their industries for future export growth.

SUMMARY OF RECOMMENDATIONS

This report recognizes the crucial importance of private-sector adjustments to improve U.S. competitiveness. Many of CED's major recommendations to both business and labor are contained in such recent statements as *Productivity Policy: Key to the Nation's Economic Future* (1983) and *Stimulating Technological Progress* (1980). The principal focus on this report is on changes in public policies that will create an environment within which the market system can flourish, in which the nation can adapt to rather than reject change, and in which we can regain and maintain a true leadership position in the world economic community.

CHAPTER 2: SOURCES AND IMPLICATIONS OF CHANGING COMPETITIVENESS

U.S. industrial competitiveness has been lost in a broad range of industries, including capital-intensive industries employing high-skilled workers — industries in which the United States has typically enjoyed a comparative advantage. Lower productivity growth rates in these industries compared to the rates of our industrial competitors have produced a convergence of productivity levels. Although the United States holds a competitive lead in some industries, this adverse trend — which has occurred over the past two decades — is cause for serious concern.

Labor costs are a major component in the production of goods and services. Since the late 1970s the difference between compensation costs in the United States and in other countries has widened. The increasing strength of the U.S. dollar has magnified the cost advantage of our competitors and weakened the U.S. competitive position further.

The private sector has a major responsibility for adjusting to loss of competitiveness. Management and employers can help restore productivity through moderating compensation growth and adopting payment systems more directly linked to productivity performance. Competitiveness can often be enhanced if management and labor recognize the importance of adapting to economic change through industrial restructuring. This includes concentrating on the high-skilled, capital-intensive phase of production and engaging in offshore assembly and production of components for those phases which are labor-intensive.

In the final analysis, competitiveness will only be maintained if U.S. businesses achieve a high rate of productivity growth through innovation. Compensation flexibility, some relocation of production to lower-cost regions within the United States and abroad are preferable to the unemployment that inevitably accompanies loss of competitiveness, but *without much higher productivity growth it will be impossible to maintain a high rate of employment growth and support improvements in real compensation.* The concern that increased trade and innovation through the application of technology to production processes will retard employment growth is understandable, but this is basically a myth. *Without increased trade over the past decade, U.S. employment growth would have been much less robust. While new technology will obviously displace some workers from their present jobs, the most serious threat to the future employment security of employees comes from failure of the enterprise to innovate.*

The government has a major role in restoring U.S. competitiveness. Its primary function is to provide the economic environment which encourages innovation in the private sector and encourages labor and capital resources to adopt to economic change. The government is also responsible for enforcing existing trade policies to prevent unfair trade practices by U.S. competitors and negotiate improvements in international trading arrangements so that all nations can compete in expanding markets on a fair basis.

CHAPTER 3: ECONOMIC AND STRATEGIC ENVIRONMENT FOR PROVIDING U.S. COMPETITIVENESS

Government policies aimed at achieving sustained, noninflationary economic growth are the basis for any set of strategies to improve U.S. competitiveness. We urge actions that will encourage such growth. This requires policies that will gradually but substantially reduce the level of projected future *federal budget deficits*.

Reducing deficits will require a further reduction in the growth of public expenditures. The size of the projected deficit will also make it necessary to raise additional revenue but it is important to avoid tax increases that discourage productive investment. Unless steps are taken to bring about a sharp reduction in budget deficits over the next few years, inflation risks will rise, capital investment will be discouraged, and the prospects of future economic growth will be impaired. Anticipation of these possibilities may already be adversely affecting investment decisions.

In order to reduce the growth of *federal expenditures*, all programs, including national defense, should be reexamined for both soundness and cost effectiveness. Although some direct program cuts may be possible, much of the future reduction in expenditures will have to come from limiting the growth of existing programs. We recommend that future benefit increases in entitlement programs (including Social Security) be less rapid than the rate of inflation while protecting the income security of the poor. We also recommend that the increase in defense buildup be less rapid than originally proposed. As the economy moves to a relatively high level of output, the long-term goal of *fiscal policy* should be to eliminate the federal deficit over the business cycle.

In general, the tax code should be reformed in ways that remove the current biases which favor consumption and discourage saving and investment. We urge consideration of some form of tax simplification that could broaden the tax base, lower rates, and provide more neutrality between incentives for individuals to consume and to save.* Business taxes should be made more neutral in the way income from different types of capital assets is taxed, and we recommend that some form of expensing (i.e., immediate deductibility of business capital investment) be considered for all plant and equipment, including research and development capital.[7]

---

7. See *Stimulating Technological Progress* (New York: CED, 1980) and *Productivity Policy: Key to the Nation's Economic Future.*

---

*See memorandum by JAMES Q. RIORDAN, page 136.

Exchange rate policy is critically important to competitiveness because, as recent experience shows, significant changes in the rate of exchange can alter the prices of U.S.-produced goods and services sold abroad and the prices of imported goods sold in the U.S. market. We urge development of an appropriate U.S. exchange rate policy that gives adequate consideration to both macroeconomic measures and other actions which may produce a more favorable exchange rate.

We encourage continued study of the practicality of government purchases and sales of foreign exchange timed to help dampen large swings in the dollar's value. Limited government operations in foreign exchange markets should be considered as these studies proceed.

National security must be a basic component of any set of industrial strategies. Much of the nation's security rests on a strong industrial base and on the ability of U.S. industry to supply basic materials in a military emergency. The government should continuously update the list of critical components for a military emergency and should estimate the national security threshold of domestic production of these components. The President, the Department of Commerce, and the Department of Defense should exercise their existing authority to stockpile strategic materials in order to meet realistic national security goals. At the same time, stockpiles of materials which are no longer necessary for national security should be gradually reduced.

Export of certain technologies can pose real security threats. We support government approval of exports if they result in a transfer of technological know-how which is truly critical to national security, but if U.S. exports to countries in the free world involve routine commodities and technical data without any effective transfer of technology, advance government approval should not be required.

CHAPTER 4: FACILITATING INDUSTRIAL, REGIONAL, AND LABOR MARKET ADJUSTMENTS

Any approach to improving U.S. competitiveness must address the issue of various types of government assistance provided to dislocated workers and to companies, industries, and regions whose competitiveness is declining.

In general, *government targeting* of domestic programs is *not* an effective mechanism for stimulating innovation, and well-intentioned subsidies to improve investment in specific industries frequently inhibit adjustment to structural change. Federal programs which provide assistance to business should not be targeted to specific companies. If future subsidies are deemed justified, they should be directed to industries rather than specific companies and should be designed to give labor and capital the time to move to other economic activities. Such assistance should be phased out according to a designated time schedule.

The federal government has an important role in contributing to the revitalization of local areas which are economically distressed, but such assistance programs should not be targeted to help specific areas of the country. Rather, we favor general programs designed to aid *any* local area in serious economic difficulty, with decisions on how such assistance should be utilized made at the local level. *Government expenditure programs* which indirectly affect the competitiveness of business should minimize distorting the flow of resources among industries.

During structural change, government can play a role in the retraining and relocation of permanently displaced workers. *Improving the efficiency and flexibility of the nation's unemployment insurance system* to encourage workers to seek new employment and to make retraining more accessible is the most effective strategy for assisting workers to adapt to economic change. In the event of *plant closings,* industries should have the flexibility to adopt voluntarily the appropriate mix of responses including prenotification, severance pay, benefit extension, and cooperation with public-sector training and relocation programs.

Ultimately, the greatest threat to employment security comes from failure of the private sector to innovate. Growth, innovation, and increased competitiveness offer far more hope for increased employment than does government protection of failing or noncompetitive industries.

CHAPTER 5: THE ROLE OF REGULATORY AND ANTITRUST POLICIES IN A COMPETITIVE STRATEGY

The government's regulation of economic activities has a direct bearing on U.S. world competitiveness. This chapter examines recent regulatory and antitrust policies and assesses the need for future changes.

In general, much *government regulation*, especially social regulation, is in need of significant reform. These reforms should concentrate on better balancing of regulation's costs and benefits, a more realistic appraisal of the effects of regulation, and the use of market incentives whenever possible.

Although fundamental changes in antitrust laws are not called for, a number of statutory and enforcement reforms are needed. In recognition of the growing interdependence of the *international economy*, all relevant government authorities should include in their analyses of market competition those firms, including foreign competitors, that are active competitors in the domestic market being analyzed. This is especially important in reviewing joint research proposals and proposed mergers. Mergers are frequently the most effective way to achieve industrial restructuring in a market economy. Unless such mergers occur there is a serious risk that pressure for protection will increase.

Congress should maintain the normal prohibition against *horizontal price-fixing* and grant exemptions only if the proposed exemption would lead to more competition and would not lead to future collusion.

We support the Justice Department's proposal to test the appropriate limits on *vertical price arrangements*. If a proper rule of reason cannot be put in place without statutory change, the Administration should submit legislation on this issue.

To streamline *antitrust enforcement*, Congress should consider broadening the precedent created by the Export Trading Act of 1982, which requires that private plaintiffs pay the cost of unsuccessful antitrust actions. In addition, extension of the clearance process created in the Export Trading Act to certain joint research ventures should be considered.

A unique aspect of U.S. antitrust litigation is the ability of injured private parties to collect automatically three times demonstrated damages. Congress should limit such triple damages to cases in which the conduct is per se illegal and carried out in secret. At the very least, judges should have discretion in multiple-damages awards.

CHAPTER 6: ADJUSTING TO CHANGING INTERNATIONAL COMPETITIVENESS

This chapter examines the responsibilities of government toward industries that are threatened by imports and the question of how to reconcile restrictive national trade actions with efficient and equitable functioning of an interdependent world economy. Many countries, including the United States, use import restrictions to protect certain domestic industries. *Escape clauses* allow the imposition of import restrictions that would otherwise not be permitted. For the United States, we recommend that granting the escape-clause protection should be treated as an unusual exception to the general policy of treating firms as risk-taking enterprises and allowing firms to succeed or fail on the basis of traditional market principles.

On a broader scale, it is vital that an effective international safeguard code be negotiated and implemented. Subjecting restrictive trade actions to international review and discipline would make it easier for all countries to resist direct protectionist measures.

There should be a long-term effort for the General Agreement on Tariffs and Trade (GATT) to restrain the growing use of foreign investment incentives and performance requirements.

A number of the more economically advanced developing countries are ready to graduate to full responsibility in the international trading community. In order to encourage this process, GATT should establish a Committee on Graduation to develop criteria to encourage the more developed Third World countries to accept the rules applying to mature international trading partners.

CHAPTER 7: UNFAIR INTERNATIONAL COMPETITION

While remedies already exist in international guidelines to deal with the problems of dumping and foreign government subsidization of exports, they should be enforced more vigorously and expeditiously than in the past.

All major countries engage in concessional financing to permit their exporting firms to gain foreign markets or protect their share of existing markets. The Organization for Economic Cooperation and Development's Agreement on Export Credits is an attempt to restrict competition among major countries by offering loans at rates substantially below market rates. In the short-run the U.S. Export-Import Bank should have sufficient resources to match below-market terms offered by foreign export credit agencies to their exporters. Where necessary, the Bank should also use its authority to blend its credits with those available from the Agency for International Development. The purpose of this short-run strategy should be to exercise leverage on all countries to agree to move toward the eventual elimination of such export credit subsidies.

When foreign governments provide their companies with domestic subsidies that do not differentiate between sales in their domestic market and sales abroad, U.S. competitiveness may be damaged by this advantage. We suggest that, although domestic subsidies are acceptable under GATT, potentially troublesome subsidies should be identified. In addition, effective remedies for subsidization affecting competition in third-country markets should be developed. New international guidelines are also needed to deal with the problems of nations targeting particular domestic industries for special assistance and support.

In dealing with *state enterprises*, if the new GATT codes on subsidies and dumping prove inadequate for dealing with abuses, special guidelines should be developed and adopted.

Nations often impose *performance requirements* on foreign-controlled companies operating in their territory. These can include minimum export levels or domestic-content requirements. New provisions for performance requirements should be negotiated to reduce those that are damaging to other countries' interests.

More effective international coordination of domestic macroeconomic policies is needed to achieve better *exchange rate equilibrium*, and International Monetary Fund (IMF) surveillance of the industrial countries' exchange rates should be strengthened. With respect to the dollar-yen exchange rate, the yen should be strengthened by further Japanese liberalization of capital inflows and encouragement of its use as an international reserve currency.*

The tax treatment of imports and exports as they enter and leave countries has long been a source of dispute among trading nations. This issue should be the subject of a comprehensive study by the OECD. Until such a study is complete and agreement on this issue is reached with our trading partners, the U.S. government should continue to provide the level of *export tax benefits* now available through the Domestic International Sales Corporation (DISC), or an equivalent replacement, but in a manner consistent with GATT principles.

CHAPTER 8: TRADE IN SERVICES

We urge this country to take the lead in reducing restrictions and establishing a stable environment for the growing international trade in services. A major goal should be the development of an *international system* for service trade and means of settling disputes in this area.

As a first step, the United States should review its own laws and regulations and revise those that discourage service exports. A midterm goal should be the establishment of a non-rule-making international body (preferably within GATT) to exchange information, settle disputes, and discourage new restrictions on service trade. The ultimate goal of these international negotiations should be to reduce barriers to service trade and to establish some international guidelines at the GATT level to govern this sector of commerce.

---

*See memorandum by JACK F. BENNETT, page 137.

Chapter 2

Sources and Implications of Changing Competitiveness

Economic growth is an uneven process, and the real growth rate of an economy is always a composite of different rates for individual sectors and industries. Progress to higher stages of economic development is almost invariably accompanied by a gradual shift in the composition of economic activity, initially from agriculture to manufacturing and later from manufacturing to a wide variety of services. Within these broad sectors, changes in the composition of output and employment also occur as some industries grow rapidly, others grow slowly or stagnate, and others decline. Indeed, the expansion of the rapid-growth industries depends partially on the release of resources from contracting industries. In short, *growth means change, and both public and private policies to promote growth must facilitate adjustment to change rather than attempt to prevent it.*

IMPORTANCE OF COMPARATIVE PERFORMANCE

Differences among countries in the relative or comparative advantages of production depend on a comparison of the structure of costs and prices of domestic products in relation to that of the same products in other countries. It is these differences in comparative advantage that make it mutually beneficial for nations to engage in trade.

Since comparative prices and costs of production can, and frequently do, change, a country can gradually lose or gain comparative advantage in specific products or industries. At any given time every country has a comparative advantage in certain products and a comparative disadvantage in others. It follows, therefore, that the concept of a loss of competitiveness or comparative advantage refers only to specific products, not to the economy as a whole.

If the *general* level of costs and prices moves out of line with those of other countries, exports will fall off, domestic demand will switch from home production to increased imports, and the current balance of trade will deteriorate, thereby reducing the *relative* competitiveness of all industries. This overall loss of international competitiveness is a macroeconomic problem and must be remedied primarily through policies designed to restore the entire economy's international competitive position. Such policies include fiscal and monetary measures to reduce overall demand and slow down cost and price increases, and an exchange-rate adjustment to alter the general relationship between domestic and foreign costs and prices. A liberal trade policy can also make an important contribution to reducing inflation by allowing the pressure of foreign competition to restrain cost and price increases.

The competitiveness of an industry depends on its costs of production and the prices of its products relative to those of other U.S. industries and to overseas competitors. An industry's cost-price structure is affected by many factors, including the costs of capital, labor, energy, and transportation as well as the scale of operations. The productivity level of the industry can play an important role in offsetting any cost disadvantage that an industry may have relative to foreign competitors. A high rate of productivity growth may not be enough to make U.S. industries more competitive than their foreign counterparts, but unless the level of productivity equals or exceeds the productivity levels of competitors in industrialized countries, it will be difficult for U.S. industries to remain competitive in world markets.

Low rates of productivity growth in the United States compared with the performance of other industrialized nations have been a chronic source of competitive weakness throughout much of U.S. industry. After two decades of lower manufacturing productivity growth rates compared with the rates achieved in several other countries, there has been a convergence of manufacturing productivity levels among the United States and its industrial competitors. On average, the U.S. and Japanese manufacturing levels have completely converged. In some industries, the United States still has the highest productivity level, but in others, such as steel and automobiles,

U.S. industry has been surpassed and has lost its former competitive lead.[1] There is no precise measure of comparative nonmanufacturing productivity levels, but consistently low productivity growth rates in many U.S. non-manufacturing industries suggest that some firms in other sectors of the economy, including services, may also risk a loss of their favorable competitive position if they do not achieve much higher rates.

In the 1983 policy statement *Productivity Policy: Key to the Nation's Economic Future*, CED analyzed the major reasons for the U.S. productivity problem. The cumulative effect of low rates of capital investment compared with higher rates in a number of other nations and insufficient innovation are reasons for an adverse trend in the average unit cost of production in many U.S. industries. These circumstances are essentially the result of U.S. private-sector and government policy decisions and have little to do with the expansion of international trade. In fact, the increased international competition that has accompanied trade liberalization has produced an important incentive for U.S. management to pay greater attention to productivity improvement. Increased trade has also encouraged resources to move from low-productivity activities to more productive uses.

Because employee compensation represents a major proportion of the cost of producing goods and services, comparative compensation levels among countries are a key determinant of an industry's competitiveness.[2]* By the end of the 1970s, the rate of increase in labor compensation was beginning to play a role in declining competitiveness of some U.S. goods and services. Figure 4 shows that during the 1960-1973 and 1973-1979 periods, despite relatively lower productivity growth rates in the United States than in other countries, on average U.S. manufacturing remained competitive in terms of unit labor cost increases. This was due to moderate increases in U.S. compensation, a favorable trend in exchange rates, and a narrowing of wage levels among industrial countries as the higher productivity growth rates of other countries permitted them to raise wages rapidly.

---

1. See William J. Baumol and Kenneth McLennan, eds., *Stimulating U.S. Productivity Growth* (New York: Oxford University Press, forthcoming 1984), Chapter 1.

---

2. The role of labor costs in the competitiveness of U.S. products has increased as the scope of markets has expanded. For example, more countries have well-developed capital markets, and differences in costs of financing are less important in determining competitiveness because international borrowing and lending to finance economic activity are now much more common. Similarly, an increase in international trade in plant and machinery, more rapid transfer of technological knowledge, and a decline in the real cost of communications and transportation have reduced the relative importance of *nonlabor* costs of production and increased the significance of comparative compensation rates as a factor in determining U.S. competitiveness. See Daniel J. B. Mitchell, "International Convergence with U.S. Wage Levels" (Paper presented at Industrial Relations Research Association Annual Meeting, San Francisco, December 1983).

---

*See memorandum by THEODORE A. BURTIS, page 137.

This trend gradually narrowed the relative *level* of manufacturing hourly labor costs among industrial countries. For example, on the basis of an index of hourly compensation, Japanese manufacturing compensation rose from 48 to 67 percent of the U.S. level of compensation between 1975 and 1978. Toward the end of the 1970s, however, the United States entered a period of rapidly rising inflation and larger average increases in annual compensation at a time when productivity growth was dropping.

As shown in Figure 4, the U.S. increase in hourly unit labor cost between 1979 and 1982 was two to three times more rapid than the increase in Japan and somewhat less than twice the increase in the Federal Republic of Germany. Moreover, the growing strength of the dollar made the loss of competitiveness in terms of unit labor costs much worse. As a result, since 1979, the differential in the levels of hourly compensation in manufacturing between the United States and its major trading partners has increased. Expressed in U.S. dollars, the Japanese compensation level has declined from 67 to 49 percent of the U.S. level. In 1978, the level of hourly compensation for the Federal Republic of Germany was higher than the U.S. level; but by 1982, compensation had dropped to 88 percent of hourly compensation in U.S. manufacturing.[3]

Accelerating compensation costs have played a crucial role in the loss of competitiveness of some U.S. industries. Indeed, the wages in such industries as steel and automobiles have been rising much more rapidly than the average for the manufacturing sector as a whole. In 1970, for example, U.S. steelworkers earned about 22 percent more than the average manufacturing workers; and in 1982, they earned 47 percent more. For autoworkers, the premium rose from 26 to 47 percent, even after the 1980-1982 slowdown in wage rate increases.[4] Moreover, these figures underestimate the actual growth in the total labor cost premium because they do not include fringe benefits; the total hourly compensation premium is now probably closer to 75 percent in both industries.

Given the cumulative effect of such large increases, *further deterioration of the competitive position of some U.S. industries can be stopped only through a combination of improved productivity, a decline in real wages, and policies that reduce the current strength of the U.S. dollar.*

---

3. These data on the index of relative hourly compensation are based on unpublished data from the U.S. Department of Labor, Bureau of Labor Statistics.

---

4. These unpublished data from the U.S. Department of Labor, Bureau of Labor Statistics, cover other workers as well as steelworkers and autoworkers, and probably underestimate the average wage premium. Primary-metal workers were used as a proxy for steelworkers; the proxy for autoworkers was workers employed in the manufacture of transportation equipment.

FIGURE 4

Average Annual Increase in Unit Labor Costs in Manufacturing for United States and Major Trading Partners, 1960 to 1982

(Percent)

	1960-1973		1973-1979		1979-1982	
	National Currency	U.S.-Dollar Basis	National Currency	U.S.-Dollar Basis	National Currency	U.S.-Dollar Basis
United States	1.9	1.9	7.2	7.2	8.0	8.0
Canada	1.8	1.9	9.3	6.1	12.1	10.1
Japan	3.5	4.9	4.3	9.7	3.1	-.7
France	3.1	2.8	9.4	9.8	12.3	-3.9
Federal Republic of Germany	3.7	6.1	4.6	11.0	5.1	-5.5
United Kingdom	4.1	2.6	17.1	12.7	12.2	4.4

SOURCE: "International Comparisons of Manufacturing Productivity and Labor Cost Trends, Preliminary Measures for 1982," *News* (Washington, D.C.: U.S. Department of Labor, Bureau of Labor Statistics, May 26, 1983).

NOTE: Average annual percentage increase is computed from the least-squares trend of the logarithms of the index numbers. The figures for the United States reflect revisions made in July 1983. Data for all other countries are based on index numbers through 1982.

EMPLOYMENT IMPLICATIONS OF
CHANGING COMPETITIVENESS

Many workers and their representatives have expressed fears that the level of employment in major sectors of the economy will be reduced as industry responds to changes in the competitive environment. Some also believe that there will be substantial erosion of the U.S. manufacturing base and that many high-wage jobs will be permanently displaced.

There is little evidence that industrial restructuring during the 1970s reduced U.S. employment growth or that the U.S. manufacturing sector is in the process of deindustrializing. On the contrary, U.S. manufacturing employment actually expanded during the 1970s, even though the *proportion* of the labor force employed in this sector continued to decline gradually. Import penetration reduced employment growth in some industries, but this was offset by increased employment through the expansion of exports in others.

A growing loss of competitiveness in some industries between 1973 and 1981 produced a negative trade balance of $7.8 billion in consumer products and $7.2 billion in automotive products. However, the increasing importance of trade resulted in substantial output growth in some industries, such as agriculture and the emerging high-technology sector. By 1981, the United States enjoyed a positive balance of about $32 billion in the export of capital goods, and the positive balance for chemicals rose to about $9 billion.[5] This made the export sector an increasingly important source of employment growth.

What was occurring within the manufacturing sector, at least up to 1980, was a gradual but significant shift of capital and labor resources toward industries with relatively high productivity and away from industries employing less skilled labor and/or manufacturing based on routine production methods in which the United States had lost its relative advantage. Without this reallocation of resources through the operation of the market system, the post-1973 decline in the overall rate of productivity growth would have been much worse.[6]

---

5. William H. Branson, "Trade and Structural Adjustment in U.S. Economy" (Draft paper prepared for conference sponsored by the American Enterprise Institute and Clark University, September 23, 1983). Since 1981 the negative trade balance in all sectors worsened as a result of the recession and the increasing strength of the dollar. For example, the negative trade balance in automotive products rose to about $17 billion in 1982.

---

6. See Frank M. Gollop, "Evidence for a Sector-Biased or Sector-Neutral Industrial Strategy: Analysis of the Productivity Slowdown," in William J. Baumol and Kenneth McLennan, eds., *Stimulating U.S. Productivity Growth*, Chapter 7.

During the process of industrial restructuring, such traditional industries as steel, automobiles, and textiles have become a less important
source of employment, but this does not mean that basic industries will no
longer be significant to the economy. Although the domestic output of these
industries may grow more slowly or even decline, resources will gradually
shift toward high-skill, high-technology types of production within each
industry. Such a restructuring has been occurring for some time in the textile
industry, with firms that utilize the most advanced technology retaining or
even improving their competitive position in world markets.

With regard to the impact of trade, foreign trade contributed to employment growth in some forty industries between 1973 and 1980 and
played a major role in the small overall growth of manufacturing jobs
during the 1970s.[7] There is no doubt that loss of competitiveness during the
1970s was a serious problem for some industries, but the sources of the
problem were primarily domestic. Without increased trade, the growth in
U.S. employment during the 1970s would have been much less robust.

The increasing strength of the U.S. dollar and the 1981-1982 recession
have, of course, substantially reduced manufacturing employment and
made it difficult for workers laid off because of industrial restructuring to
move to other jobs. Lower interest rates and a reduction of the value of the
dollar would improve the competitive position of all U.S. industries. But
even with an improvement in the exchange rate, such industries as autos
and steel would still fall far short of restoring lost jobs because most of their
decline in competitiveness is the result of rising unit production costs and a
shift in domestic demand. Future employment levels in these industries will
depend on a sustained economic recovery and on the type of adjustment
strategy individual companies use to regain competitiveness.

PRIVATE-SECTOR RESPONSIBILITIES FOR
RESTORING COMPETITIVENESS

Reducing employment is not the only adjustment option available to
firms facing an adverse competitive environment. Most companies follow a
restructuring strategy that combines slower growth in employment (or
gradual reduction of the work force) with an absolute or relative reduction

---

7. See Robert Z. Lawrence, "Is Trade Deindustrializing America?: A Medium-Term Perspective," in
Brookings Papers on Economic Activity Issue 1, William C. Brainard and George L. Perry, eds.,
(Washington, D.C.: The Brookings Institution,), pp. 129-161.

in wage levels. Where feasible, relocating production facilities to areas where the cost of production is lower is an additional option.[8]

In the future, U.S. businesses, in labor-intensive or mature routine manufacturing are likely to lose comparative advantage to newly industrializing countries. It is important for management and labor to recognize the need to shift resources to high-skilled, capital-intensive production processes within these industries and to participate in intraindustry trade by importing intermediate products involving standardized production. This form of intraindustry trade is well advanced in the production of automobiles, where U.S. manufacturers now trade actively with the automobile industries in other countries and some of the components used in U.S. assembly operations come from foreign sources. Similarly, for products requiring labor-intensive assembly, it is to the advantage of U.S. industry to manufacture technologically advanced components domestically and assemble the final product in countries that have a large, low-cost labor supply and are located close to overseas markets.*

Offshore assembly and sourcing of components by U.S. firms is a form of imports that has accounted for about 6 percent of all imports since 1978 but in absolute terms has expanded gradually with the growth of international trade.[9] This form of intraindustry trade is essential if many U.S. manufactured goods are to compete internationally. Without it, many U.S. jobs would be lost to foreign competitors.[10]

In a market economy, management is responsible for repositioning the firm's resources and changing its product lines within the dynamic competitive environment. More important, as CED emphasized in *Productivity Policy: Key to the Nation's Economic Future*, management and labor have a

---

8. For example, the slight decline in employment in the apparel industry since 1960 was accompanied by a substantial redistribution of employment away from the Northeast to the South and the West. During the 1960s, the household appliance, electric, lighting, communication equipment, and electronic components industries underwent substantial economic change in which the most important adjustment technique was a decline in relative wages. The successful restructuring of these industries was assisted substantially by productivity growth, and during the 1970s, the relative wage trend was reversed and eventually surpassed the previous peak in each industry. See Ann C. Orr and James A. Orr, "Employment Adjustments in Import-Sensitive Manufacturing Industries, 1960-1980" (Paper presented at the Industrial Relations Research Association Annual Meeting, San Francisco, December 1983).

---

9. See U.S. International Trade Commission, *Imports Under Items 806.30 and 807.00 of the Tariff Schedules of the United States* (Washington, D.C.: U.S. Government Printing Office, 1982).

---

10. It is estimated that during the 1973-1977 period, such trade actually produced a small growth in the number of jobs, about 200,000 jobs annually. See Report of the Secretary-General, *The Impact of the New Industrializing Countries on Production and Trade in Manufactures* (Paris: Organization for Economic Cooperation and Development, 1979).

---

*See memorandum by J.W. McSWINEY, page 138.

responsibility to increase productivity through improved cost and quality control, a compensation structure designed to reward employee innovation, and investment in research and development and in new plant and equipment to achieve technological leadership.[11]

Although the introduction of new technology frequently results in the displacement of specific workers and specific tasks, overall productivity improvement through innovation has not typically reduced employment industry-wide. Greater productivity usually permits industry to reduce its relative costs and prices sufficiently to increase demand and create more jobs than the number of jobs lost through the substitution of machinery for workers.[12]

There is considerable debate about the long-run employment effect of more rapid innovation. No matter how important innovation is to future employment growth, it will continue to cause short-run displacement of workers from specific jobs. The decisions of management and labor at the industry and company levels will largely determine how quickly and successfully these workers are reemployed. *But the most serious risk of job displacement is not from technology that is introduced too fast but from technology that is introduced too late or is never adopted.*[13]

GOVERNMENT RESPONSIBILITIES FOR RESTORING COMPETITIVENESS

Government's first responsibility is to create an overall economic environment that encourages the private sector to improve the economy's competitiveness through greater productivity.* Without macroeconomic policies to achieve noninflationary economic growth, microeconomic policies will do little to improve the competitiveness of U.S. industry.

---

11. See *Productivity Policy: Key to the Nation's Economic Future*, Chapter 6.

---

12. See Robert A. Levy, Marianne Bowes, James Jondrow, "Technical Change and Employment in Five Industries," in Eileen L. Collins and Lucretia Dewey-Tanner, eds., *American Jobs and the Changing Industrial Base* (Boston, Mass.: Ballinger, forthcoming 1984). This study analyzes innovations in the steel, automobile, aluminum, coal, and iron ore industries over the 1959-1977 period. It concludes that although innovations have a positive effect on industry employment, the actual level of employment may fall because other factors such as an increase in wages and changes in scale of operations may have a negative effect on employment growth.

---

13. See Frank P. Doyle and Kenneth McLennan, "Labor Management Policies and Industrial Competitiveness" (Paper prepared for Conference on Employment Growth in the Context of Structural Change, Organization for Economic Cooperation and Development, Paris, February 6-8, 1984).

---

*See memorandum by CLIFTON R. WHARTON, Jr., page 138.

Under the market system, whenever an industry experiences increased demand or develops new products or production processes, the market recognizes the potential for greater profitability and capital and labor resources flow into the industry. An efficiently operating market system automatically separates winners from losers. The central thrust of government's strategy should be to improve the efficiency with which markets allocate resources. This implies that government policy should remove current interventions which inhibit competition or are no longer necessary.

Some policy makers, especially in Congress, believe that during a period of industrial restructuring the government should try to moderate the pace of structural change by providing industries with temporary protection from foreign competition or with subsidies for modernization. In the United States, several companies have been rescued from failure by these types of government interventions. *Such assistance should be an exception within any government strategy to improve competitiveness and should be judged on demonstrated efforts to regain competitiveness.*

Temporary protection against imports does provide management with time to increase capital investment and reduce unit costs of production. In the short run, some jobs are obviously saved; but over a period of several years, protection does not generate any net growth in employment. Indeed, it is likely to lead to a net loss of jobs in the long run.

If temporary protection becomes permanent, it increases the cost of products to consumers, stifles overall economic growth, and slows the generation of new jobs. In our highly interdependent economy, if the protected industry's output is an intermediate product for other U.S. industries, protection will destroy more jobs than it saves. Extended protection of industries in the traditional industrial base will simply lead to a loss of competitiveness in other industries and failure to expand employment in high-technology industries, which have contributed so importantly to employment growth through exports to rapidly expanding world markets.[14]

A market-oriented strategy to improve U.S. competitiveness relies heavily on the incentives of relatively free competition to stimulate innovation. Under this strategy, firms sometimes fail. Government's role should not be to prevent failure but to facilitate the adjustment of labor resources to other employment opportunities when failure occurs.

Because the U.S. government now intervenes heavily in some markets, some proponents of an "industrial policy" argue that the United States

---

14. For an empirical study of the industries that would lose jobs from protection of basic industries, see Clapper Almon, Margaret Buckler, and Douglas Nyhus, "The Inforum Interindustry Macro Model with an Application to the Effects of Protection" (Baltimore: University of Maryland, Mimeographed, 1983).

is, in fact, already targeting specific industries. Our international competitors claim that U.S. defense policy is an example of industrial targeting that provides us with an advantage in international trade.

But targeting exists only when government explicitly directs resources into, or out of, selected industries with the intention of making them more competitive.[15] The United States has rarely followed this strategy in its policies toward industry. Some countries, during their early stages of economic development, have used a variety of targeting techniques to assist "infant" industries. Initially, this appears relatively harmless to the international marketplace. But when rapidly developing countries continue to use such practices, and when governments in highly industrialized countries use targeting techniques to improve future export growth, the welfare of citizens in other countries is likely to be reduced.

Like all other countries, the United States has a broad range of special tax arrangements, subsidies, and expenditure programs that affect industry. Individually, many of these programs indirectly affect the competitive position of specific industries. Similarly, special tax arrangements and subsidies can indirectly improve productivity in some industries. The overall impact of these interventions on U.S. productivity is difficult to estimate. General tax policies which reduce the cost of capital are desirable incentives to encourage investment in plant and equipment. If, in addition, however, special tax arrangements are targeted to specific industries the result may be more favorable tax treatment of income for some industries. More resources will flow from those economic activities which do not receive such favorable tax treatment, thus reducing the overall rate of productivity growth. *A strategy for improving competitiveness should remove tax and subsidy distortions by making these policies as neutral as possible.*

Similarly, as the discussion of competitive performance and defense expenditures makes clear, large government expenditures for national security do not constitute a targeting strategy and are not an efficient way of improving the competitiveness of U.S. industries. (See "Defense Expenditures: A Public Good or A Targeted Industrial Policy?" page 31.)

---

15. The instruments of targeting include *protection of the home market* through import quotas, tariffs, government procurement, control over the availability of foreign exchange, and prohibition against foreign investment; *tax benefits* to encourage mergers, joint ventures, and exports; *antitrust exemptions* to permit the formation of cartels, import and export consortia, and joint research and development (R and D) associations; *innovation policies* such as control over licensing of foreign technology, tax write-offs for specific R and D government purchasing and leasing of specific technology; and *direct financial assistance* such as grants, preferential loans, and easier access to foreign exchange.

The U.S. policy response to the targeting practices of other governments is an essential component of any competitiveness strategy. In the past, Japan has used targeting extensively and has made protection of the home market a top priority, although this has declined substantially since 1965. Japanese targeting of industries for future export growth through protection of the home market continues to be one of the major trading issues associated with the large trade deficit the United States has with Japan. Although much of the responsibility for this deficit is attributable to poor U.S. productivity performance, Japan still protects industries in which the United States has a comparative advantage. For example, quotas exist for some forest and agriculture products such as wood paneling, paper products, fruit, livestock, and leather. Similarly, while Japan's average tariff on manufactured goods is scheduled to decline substantially, high tariffs and nontariff barriers remain on some items, including computers, computer parts, computer peripherals, heavy electrical machinery, and medical and diagnostic equipment.

This type of targeting restricts the ability of the United States to concentrate its resources on the production of goods and services in which it has a comparative advantage. It also leads to pressure in the United States to protect industries in which Japan has a comparative advantage. *This form of industrial policy is ultimately detrimental to the interests of all nations.*

As more countries become industrialized, more countries are relying on the same high-technology industries for export growth. But multilateral reliance on the same industries need not reduce U.S. employment growth *provided world markets are expanding sufficiently.* For many U.S. industries, their share of world market has declined; yet, output and employment in these industries have expanded because markets have grown rapidly, and all nations have benefited from an increase in intraindustry trade.[16] However, if governments continue to target industries by protecting their home markets, subsidizing their industries for export growth, or negotiating collusive nontariff barriers, the spread of protectionism will retard international trade and employment growth in all countries.

Government's use of such targeting instruments threatens the expansion of world trade and not only will slow employment growth in industrial-

---

16. Relatively free markets in different countries can also result in the concentration of substantial resources in the same industries. For example, in the United States and other major industrialized countries, over 70 percent of *business-funded* R and D is concentrated in five sectors: electrical, electronic and equipment components, chemicals and drugs, aircraft, and motor vehicles. See Rolf Piekarz, Eleanor Thomas, and Donna Jennings, "International Comparison of Research and Development and Government Policies" (Paper presented at American Enterprise Institute Conference on International Comparisons of Productivity and Causes of the Slowdown, Washington, D.C., October 1982).

ized countries, but also will make domestic adjustment to structural change more difficult. Despite strong pressure within all countries to pursue policies that produce winning industries, governments must negotiate improvements in international trading arrangements so that all nations can compete in expanding markets on a fair basis. This should be a major goal of trade policy within a U.S. strategy to improve competitiveness.

DEFENSE EXPENDITURES: A PUBLIC GOOD OR A TARGETED INDUSTRIAL POLICY?

Government funding of defense expenditures is necessary because there is no incentive for individuals or groups to make such expenditures on their own. Our competitors often claim that the large U.S. expenditures on defense represent government targeting to improve the competitiveness of U.S. industries in international markets. But since the benefits of defense are widely dispersed through the population it is a public good, not government targeting.

All nations use direct expenditures, loans, loan guarantees, and special tax arrangements to meet goals that benefit society. Some industries will benefit from this form of assistance, but that does not mean the government is targeting assistance to make those industries more competitive. For example, in 1980, 68 percent of all higher education expenditures in the United States was publicly funded. This increases the demand for institutions within the higher education sector above what it would have been without government support. Many employers in the United States, as well as some employers in other countries, also benefit from an increase in the supply of highly skilled workers, but the primary intended beneficiaries are the recipients of higher education. The purpose of public expenditures for education is not to raise the income of specific educational institutions or reduce the cost of skilled labor to employers in particular industries. Public expenditures to support higher education are necessary because, in part, the output (e.g., basic research and the benefits of an educated population) is a public good. For the most part, however, these expenditures are intended to provide U.S. citizens (and foreign students) with an opportunity to increase their well-being and provide benefits to society generally.

Defense expenditures also affect the demand for some industries more than others, and there are some commercial spin-offs from defense expenditures that benefit U.S. firms. But research is inconclusive on whether these benefits to the nondefense sector of the economy are worth their costs. Defense expenditures are primarily a public good to increase national security. *Because the primary beneficiaries of U.S. defense expenditures are U.S. citizens and their allies, these expenditures do not constitute a targeted industrial policy.*

32

Chapter 3

Economic and Strategic Environment for Promoting U.S. Competitiveness

The CED approach to improving the competitiveness of the economy emphasizes macroeconomic policies to achieve stable, noninflationary economic growth. Without such policies, microeconomic policies to improve the operation of markets will have little effect.

MACROECONOMIC ISSUES IN A COMPETITIVE STRATEGY

Government monetary and fiscal policies greatly affect a nation's ability to realize the benefits of structural change through productivity growth, technological innovation, and increased international trade. The tax and spending policies of the government and the monetary operations of the Federal Reserve System affect the level of output, employment, and the overall rate of price increases in the economy. The rate of productivity growth for the economy as a whole will be increased if output and employment can be raised without high rates of inflation. But simultaneously achieving these macroeconomic goals is difficult, as has been demonstrated by the coexistence of significant inflation and unemployment during several periods since World War II. Nevertheless, progress — uneven but considerable — has recently been made. Since the unemployment rate peaked in 1982, output and employment have expanded rapidly through the first stage of the recovery from the 1981-1982 recession. The rate of inflation has fallen dramatically and appears to have stabilized at a relatively low rate.

But increased output and employment may not be sustained through the decade unless real progress is made toward reducing the huge federal deficits that are now being projected through the late 1980s. The solution is not increased government borrowing because this would only preempt a substantial proportion of net individual saving. If the demand for private borrowing expands while government borrowing is increasing, interest rates may rise, and some private investment could be crowded out. One of the more insidious effects might be to bias private-sector investment toward short-term projects and away from those with longer-term payoffs. Large deficits and relatively high real interest rates in the United States also attract foreign funds, elevate the dollar exchange rate, and put upward pressure on interest rates in other countries, thus making it more difficult to expand U.S. exports.

Uncertainty about the projected level of deficits and whether continued high interest rates will eventually choke off the economic recovery may already be slowing economic growth to some extent.[1] No country can continue for long to increase its expenditures for interest on debt at a rate higher than that of economic growth without eventually reducing the growth of the private business sector.[2]

Some of the uncertainty that now affects business investment decisions would be diminished by adopting policies that would gradually but significantly reduce the magnitude of the out-year budget deficits. Unless comprehensive and forceful steps are taken by the Administration and Congress to bring about a large reduction in the budget deficits over the 1985-1988 period, the prospects for a sustained recovery could be impaired, and the competitive position of U.S. industries would be diminished further.

---

1. See Craig Elwell, *Are High Interest Rates a Threat to Sustained Economic Recovery?* (Washington, D.C.: U.S. Library of Congress, Congressional Research Service, July 1983).

---

2. The problem is related primarily to the structural components of the deficit, which can be expected to remain even after the economy has moved back toward relatively high levels of capacity utilization and employment. Some actual budget deficits at a time when the economy is still operating well below capacity may in fact be required to sustain the recovery. The notion of gearing fiscal policy to a balanced budget or a surplus at an assumed high level of employment was developed by CED in 1948. See the policy statements *Taxes and the Budget: A Program for Prosperity and a Free Economy* (New York: CED, 1947) and *Strengthening the Federal Budget Process: A Requirement for Effective Fiscal Control* (New York: CED, 1983). The issue of economic stabilization will be reviewed in a forthcoming CED policy statement on economic stabilization and growth.

MICROECONOMIC IMPLICATIONS OF FISCAL POLICIES

In recent policy statements, CED has pointed out that unless the nation reverses the bias toward current public and private consumption and stimulates more capital investment, U.S. productivity performance will fail to match that of other major industrialized nations. This will then pose a serious problem for the competitiveness of many U.S. industries in international markets and will make a higher standard of living for all groups in society more difficult to achieve.[3] *The long-run goal of fiscal policy should be to eliminate progressively the structural component of the deficit as the economy moves to a relatively high level of output.*[4]

REDUCING FEDERAL EXPENDITURES

Making the transition to a more balanced budget involves the difficult choice of whether to cut expenditures, raise taxes, or both.[5] We believe that the growth of federal expenditures can be cut by reexamining the purpose, soundness, and cost effectiveness of all programs, including those related to national defense. However, given the size of the projected budget, improved program efficiency is unlikely to produce savings sufficient to bring about a significant reduction in the out-year deficits. Because entitlement programs, including Social Security, represent such a large share of federal expenditures, it will undoubtedly be necessary to reduce the rate of benefit increases, especially for those programs whose beneficiaries are not poor.[6] This approach will gradually reduce the current consumption bias in public expenditures. Similarly, although we support a substantial increase in defense spending, we believe that defense goals could be achieved through a combination of more efficient use of resources and a somewhat less rapid defense buildup.

---

3. See the policy statements *Redefining Government's Role in the Market System* (New York: CED, 1979), and *Productivity Policy: Key to the Nation's Economic Future.*

---

4. For a discussion of the importance of reducing this structural component of the budget deficit and how the congressional budget process can be improved to achieve this goal, see the policy statement *Strengthening the Federal Budget Process: A Requirement for Effective Fiscal Control.*

---

5. The potential for slowing the growth of expenditures depends in part upon the past and future trends in expenditures. Over the 1965-1980 period, nondefense expenditures grew at an annual rate of about 13 percent while defense expenditures expanded at 9 percent per annum. Over that period, defense outlays had declined to 24 percent of total outlays, compared with 40 percent in 1965. Since 1980, these trends have been reversed. Defense expenditures are projected to grow more rapidly through 1986, but nondefense expenditures will increase at an annual rate of about 8.5 percent. See William Cox, *Budget Deficits: Causes, Effects and Some Remedial Options* (Washington, D.C.: U.S. Library of Congress, Congressional Research Service, June 1983).

REFORMING THE INDIVIDUAL AND CORPORATE TAX SYSTEMS

The early 1980s have seen major changes in U.S. tax policy. The Economic Recovery Tax Act of 1981 (ERTA) substantially reduced marginal and average individual tax rates, but increases in Social Security taxes and continued "tax bracket creep" largely negated the act's intended overall tax reduction. ERTA did provide a potential stimulus to investment in plant and equipment, but some of this effect was taken back with the passage of the Tax Equity and Fiscal Responsibility Act of 1982 (TEFRA). The stimulus was also undercut by higher real interest rates than in previous recessions.

ERTA included new provisions to encourage individual saving, somewhat reducing the proconsumption bias in the tax code. We have previously pointed out that this type of policy change was one of the necessary conditions for encouraging investment to enhance long-run productivity performance.[7]

However, the large reduction in individual taxes in 1981 was not accompanied by enough reductions in federal expenditures to avoid a growing federal deficit. Furthermore, federal revenues have been substantially reduced by the effects of the 1981-1982 recession because high unemployment rates have meant that fewer persons have paid income and Social Security taxes while more have collected from such income-maintenance programs as unemployment compensation. Once the economy has fully recovered from the recession, tax and expenditure policies need to ensure that there is sufficient revenue to finance public investment in the type of capital assets which enhance productivity growth and finance realistic social goals.

---

6. Social Security and related health programs are the largest entitlement programs, accounting for 27 to 30 percent of federal expenditures. As one method of ensuring the long-term solvency of the Social Security system, CED's Program Committee has suggested that automatic cost-of-living increases be limited to less than 100 percent of the increase in the Consumer Price Index (CPI), perhaps to 60 or 80 percent. See the CED program statement *Social Security: From Crisis to Crisis?* (New York: CED, 1984). Only about 10 percent of the elderly who receive Social Security retirement income are now defined as poor. If Social Security benefit increases are limited to less than the CPI this would gradually increase the proportion of the elderly receiving Social Security retirement income who are classifed as poor. However, this estimate of poverty among the elderly is misleading since it is measured on the basis of *before* tax income and does not take account of non-cash benefits or family sizes. The relative income of the elderly is about the same as the non-elderly population when measured by *after* tax income per person. See "Estimating After Tax Money Income Distributions," *Current Populations Reports*, no. 126 (Washington, D.C.: U.S. Department of Commerce, Bureau of the Census, 1983).

The most efficient way to increase the income of the elderly poor is to increase benefits under the Supplemental Security Income program (SSI) which, unlike the Social Security retirement income program, is a means-tested anti-poverty program. See U.S. House of Representatives, Committee on Ways and Means, *Background Material on Poverty* (Washington, D.C.: U.S. Government Printing Office, 1983), p. 90.

---

7. See *Productivity Policy: Key to the Nation's Economic Future*, Chapter 5.

The present individual tax code is an extremely complicated patchwork of special tax preferences that is almost incomprehensible to the average taxpayer. For the long run, CED favors moving toward an alternative approach to taxing individuals. Major reform of the tax code could be achieved through a significant reduction in these tax preferences. Such a reform would broaden the tax base and thereby permit a further significant reduction in average and marginal tax rates and would at the same time preserve a moderate degree of progressivity. This approach would reduce the debilitating influence of tax considerations on personal decisions, achieve more neutrality between incentives for individuals to consume and to save, and contribute to productivity growth.[8]

ERTA and TEFRA permitted business to write off the cost of capital investment more rapidly. These changes in the capital recovery system will increase the rate of investment in new plant and equipment and contribute to productivity growth. The stimulus to investment in new plant and equipment will be greatest toward the end of the decade because investment has been delayed by the recent recession and the existence of excess capacity. Some preliminary estimates indicate that the combined effect of the new depreciation schedules and the liberalized investment tax credit will be a 2.5 to 14.0 percent increase in the U.S. capital stock by the end of the decade.[9]

We strongly support the basic thrust of recent tax policy changes designed to stimulate capital investment by reducing the cost of capital. While the federal government should be prepared to increase tax revenues, as well as to make significant expenditure cuts, it is important to avoid the types of tax increases that discourage overall investment in new plant and equipment.

In the policy statement *Productivity Policy: Key to the Nation's Economic Future*, we pointed out that the current incentive to new capital investment is not neutral among different types of assets. This has distorted the allocation of capital resources among industries and between plant structures and equipment. The distortion has been magnified by the growth of special business tax incentives designed to achieve particular goals, including a reduction in the heavier burden of regulatory restrictions on some industries than on others. As a result, there is considerable disparity in

8. See *Productivity Policy: Key to the Nation's Economic Future*, pp. 48-53. For a more detailed evaluation of the weaknesses of the current income tax system, see Congressional Budget Office, *Revising the Individual Income Tax* (Washington, D.C.: U.S. Government Printing Office, July 1983).

9. Martin David, Robert Haveman, and Stephen Oliver, *The Economic Recovery Tax Act of 1981: An Early Assessment of its Effects on Business Innovation* (Madison, Wis.: Mimeographed, 1982).

tax rates among industries, and this encourages new investment in plant and equipment to flow more readily to those industries with the most favorable tax treatment. We believe that expensing (immediately writing off) of capital investment (including R and D) by business should be considered as an option for inclusion in the long-run strategy to enhance the competitiveness of U.S. industry. The revenue loss from such expensing of capital investment could be offset by trading many of the special tax preferences for business for a reduction in the statutory corporate tax rate. The corporate tax code could be designed to produce the same revenue, but it would be much more neutral because most firms would be taxed at a much lower statutory rate.[10]

In implementing some form of expensing, it is important not to penalize firms in cyclically sensitive industries. Any reforms of the corporate tax structure should attempt to be countercyclical so that they contribute to macroeconomic goals.

EXCHANGE RATE POLICY

Exchange rates directly affect the prices of U.S.-produced goods and services sold abroad and also the prices of foreign goods sold in U.S. markets.

Nations have resorted to a variety of policies for establishing, defending and influencing exchange rates. For the past decade, following the breakdown of the post-World War II effort to maintain a system of governmentally fixed exchange rates among the world's major currencies, the United States has generally allowed the exchange value of the dollar to float in the exchange markets — that is, to move up and down with the total of market transactions in dollars. Under this flexible system, the strength and freedom of private market-making forces have grown, and so has the volume of transactions. The markets of the major trading and financial countries have become more interdependent than ever before.

With relatively free international movements of funds, transfers from one currency to another are not limited to payments for currently produced goods and services or transfers of current savings; they also potentially include the huge total of accumulated past savings — the world's wealth, in effect. When the incentives to move large amounts of these accumulated assets (and liabilities) from one country to another become strong, as they

---

10. See *Productivity Policy: Key to the Nation's Economic Future*, pp. 54-57. A CED Design Committee on Tax Policy is currently working on an extensive review of the tax code, including a more detailed analysis of a wide range of options to improve tax policy.

are today, the resulting fund transfers (and expected transfers) can dominate exchange transactions based on current trade and services and can push currency exchange rates to levels markedly different from those that would balance current production costs among the various trading countries.

Various conditions can lead to such large capital transfers, including big new discoveries of valuable natural resources or widespread doubts about the political stability or financial soundness of countries. Large and sustained differences in interest rate levels between countries, resulting from mismatches in fiscal and monetary policies, both in and between countries, can also induce large international capital movements. That prospect can produce significant changes in exchange rates.

Short-run movements in exchange rates are inevitable, but a long-run misalignment in rates cannot be tolerated if it changes the basic competitiveness of U.S. industry.* From 1979 through 1983, the United States experienced such a misalignment with a strongly rising exchange rate for the dollar. The chief contributor to this policy mismatch has been the emergence of exceptionally large federal budget deficits. The resulting combination of relatively high real interest rates and a sustained strong exchange rate has created profound changes in the international competitiveness of many U.S. firms. *In effect, the U.S. government has produced a noncompetitive macroeconomic environment that has seriously worsened the international competitiveness of U.S. industry.*

The side effects of this fiscal-monetary mismatch have been far greater than generally foreseen or desired. On the plus side, the dollar's relatively high exchange rate has lowered the cost of imports and thus helped to moderate U.S. inflation. In addition, the inflow of foreign capital has kept U.S. interest rates from being even higher. But the negative effects have been severe. U.S. producers trying to sell in competition with foreign producers have suffered from a relatively higher real cost of financing than some international competitors who can borrow in their domestic currency at lower interest rates.

Most important, the dollar's unusually strong exchange rate has persisted long enough to inflict a major price handicap on many U.S. producers, resulting in major losses in sales, market position, jobs, and profits in some industries. In many cases, these operational curtailments, worker layoffs, and plant closings have been forced much faster or much further than is called for to achieve the most efficient use of the world's human and physical resources. In fact, the process often seems to have gone so far as to hurt seriously those U.S. producers whose long-run competitive position is sensitive to unfavorable fluctuations in exchange rates. Since the U.S.

---

*See memorandum by JOHN B. CAVE, page 139.

THE ROLE OF EXCHANGE RATES IN INFLUENCING TRADE FLOWS AND CAPITAL MOVEMENTS

If no net capital movements take place, exchange rates between currencies adjust to balance the overall values of goods and services moving among countries in international trade. In the process, the prices of similar, tradable goods tend to be equalized across national boundaries. Under competitive conditions, domestic firms must match the price and quality of goods available from foreign producers or lose sales to them. Hence, when the home currency strengthens enough against one or more foreign currencies, it can force domestic firms to increase their efficiency, shift to more profitable lines of business, or go out of business completely. If all works ideally, each country will tend to concentrate its output in those fields in which it is relatively most efficient and thereby tend to maximize the overall income it earns over the long run through production.

This kind of adjustment mechanism can also work to balance current saving and investing among countries. Citizens in a country with a high net saving rate and relatively few profitable current investment opportunities will find it worthwhile to lend some portion of their current savings to finance plant and equipment outlays in foreign countries with relatively profitable investment opportunities and relatively low domestic saving. This adjustment mechanism can also work with respect to transfers of previously accumulated capital among countries when such capital moves to a more productive and profitable use elsewhere. These capital movements modify exchange rates enough to balance the combined total value of goods and services and capital movements among countries. As exchange rates move to new levels, however, those firms that become the relatively least efficient producers will tend to lose sales to their foreign competitors.

As these adjustments take place, they may be accompanied by significant transitional costs, including loss of jobs and output. They will, however, tend to lead to the most efficient production patterns and greatest consumer satisfaction in the long run. But an exception to this general rule occurs when exchange rates are affected by forces external to the market, such as political changes, or financial signals that do not reflect underlying economic relationships. In this case, adjustment costs are higher and tend to be distributed disproportionately. Moreover, if the distortions are protracted, a less efficient use of resources may result.

dollar is the principle currency of international exchange, it has also encouraged the flow of capital in a way that is probably harmful to other countries' economies. **In our judgment, such extensive damage to the industrial structure is so adverse to the long-run interests of the United States that it deserves to be a major consideration in the shaping of U.S. fiscal and monetary policies. The same is true for the monetary and fiscal policies of our major trading partners.**

History teaches us not to expect that the dollar will always be strong in the international exchange markets. As recently as the late 1970s, a different combination of circumstances and policies, including the succession of oil price increases by the Organization of Petroleum Exporting Countries (OPEC), led to a much lower exchange value for the dollar against some other major currencies. But the longer the current fiscal-monetary mismatch continues to hold up real interest rates and the dollar's exchange rate, the greater the damage will be to U.S. industry.

If the international competitiveness of U.S. firms were to be the sole criterion, the best monetary-fiscal mix would usually be one that is sufficiently balanced to keep real U.S. interest rates from being forced far out of line relative to those of our major industrial competitors. There would also be a need for more effective multilateral consultation among the chief industrial nations aimed at closer coordination of monetary and fiscal policies.[11]

In practice, however, other powerful national considerations can sometimes bear heavily on the determination of fiscal and monetary policies, such as those that have given rise to the current high federal deficits, restrained growth of some monetary aggregates, and relatively high real interest rates. Because these other considerations can result in a fiscal-monetary mix that is far from ideal for U.S. competitiveness, the nation needs to face squarely the question of whether there are any other measures that could moderate the damaging exchange rate side effects of the mismatch. For similar reasons, we should also address the usual swings in the exchange value of the dollar that reflect major changes in the demand for dollar assets for safe-haven reasons (i.e., because of fears about the political or financial stability of various countries). Such safe-haven flows appear to be an important force adding to the dollar's current strength from 1979 through 1983.

Any call for U.S. action on exchange rates should recognize the practical limitations on what such measures can accomplish. There was a

---

11. For further discussion of the need for international coordination of macroeconomic policies, see page 115.

time during and after World War II when many countries used direct controls to constrain the volume of international capital flows across their borders. Experience demonstrated, however, that such capital controls could be damaging to both economic efficiency and economic freedom. Moreover, capital controls have become increasingly ineffective in many countries with the rapid rise in the volume and sophistication of international capital movements. This is particularly true of the United States, as it has grown into the role of the world financial capital.

Most major governments have resorted to a more market-oriented technique to try to affect their currencies' international exchange rates; that is, direct or indirect purchases or sales of foreign currencies in foreign exchange markets. The efficacy of this technique is limited by the increasing interdependence of financial markets among the trading countries. Indeed, if such interdependence were to proceed to its logical conclusion, the result would be perfectly integrated world financial markets in which all borrowers of equal risk could borrow on equal real terms. In such a world, government transactions in the foreign exchange (or other financial) markets would be unable to create distinctively different national financial conditions.

But the world has not yet reached this point of market perfection. In the present circumstances, it seems possible for the right kind of government activity in foreign exchange markets to dampen, although probably only to a mild degree, undesirably large swings in the dollar's value in those markets stemming from mismatched fiscal and monetary policies or safe-haven capital movements.[12]

Deciding whether, when, and how best to conduct such foreign exchange market activity involves complicated technical questions. Some light was cast on these questions by the recent report of an intergovernmental working group established at the 1982 Summit Conference.[13] **But enough operational issues remain unclear so that they deserve continued careful study, even as limited government operations in the foreign exchange markets proceed.** This study needs to be pursued by the appropriate government authorities with input from private-sector experts.

---

12. The kind of foreign exchange operations by government being examined in this section should be distinguished from those short-term crisis-type interventions designed to forestall a breakdown in market functioning. Precedents for such operations have already been worked out by the United States (although it is difficult to judge how helpful they will be in such hard-to-predict situations). In contrast, the industrial damage discussed here typically results from an exaggerated swing of the dollar exchange rate that persists over months or years.

---

13. *Report of the Working Group on Exchange Market Intervention* (Washington, D.C.: Publications Services, Board of Governors of the Federal Reserve System, Mimeographed, March 1983).

42

We need also to probe for and test other ideas for policies, institutions, or instruments that might help to dampen exchange rate swings that go far beyond the levels needed to balance the costs of goods and services traded. The industrial damage that can be done by such excessive and prolonged shifts in exchange rates is simply too great to be tolerated.

Both for this occasion and for similar occasions in the future, we believe the development of an appropriate U.S. exchange rate policy is needed, whether implemented through adaptations in macro-economic policies, foreign exchange market operations, or other appropriate measures.

The effort being called for here should not be confused with the review of the entire world monetary system being called for in some quarters (often under the label of a "new Bretton Woods conference"). That is an undertaking of still greater scope and complexity, and in view of the changed conditions that have evolved in the postwar decades and the attendant alterations in people's thinking, the appropriate time for it may be drawing close. But for such a conference to succeed, a great deal of careful preparatory work is needed, and this preparation deserves to be pressed forward now. Among other prerequisites, there needs to be a greater appreciation of the fact that no world monetary system can relieve governments, businesses, and individuals of the need to adapt to substantial and sustained changes in relative prices and costs.

NATIONAL SECURITY

Improving the competitiveness of U.S. industry is essential if the United States is to maintain its military and political leadership position in the world. U.S. national security depends on a highly productive and diversified industrial structure. A highly competitive economy is essential to the efficient production of up-to-date goods and services for both civilian and military purposes.*

Achieving the benefits of structural change raises several national security issues. If the results of economic change are increased trade and more specialization of production among nations, the United States may come to rely heavily on other nations for materials critical to its own defense. As international competition and trade increase, it is possible that the capacity of some U.S. industries will gradually decline. If this decline is substantial, national security will become an issue. And if it occurs in an industry critical to military preparedness, it will become a very serious issue indeed.

*See memorandum by FRAZAR B. WILDE, page 139.

National security must always be taken into consideration in any approach to developing an industrial and competitive strategy. The Defense Production Act of 1950 as extended authorizes the federal government to subsidize the domestic production of critical materials. In general, however, we believe it is preferable to stockpile materials and identify the cost as part of the Defense Department budget. This avoids the problem of estimating the costs of loans and guarantees, and it is more consistent with reducing the growth of government intervention in the economy.

This Administration has initiated steps to strengthen the reserves of critical materials. In order to avoid unnecessary costs in the future, **the current procedure for developing and meeting security needs should be fully implemented, whereby the decision to continue stockpiling of critical material is reaffirmed by the President every three years on the basis of an evaluation report prepared through an interagency stockpile review. The government should implement a gradual phaseout, over a period of several years, of the stockpiled material that is no longer critical to national security.**

Although stockpiling can take care of much of the nation's defense material needs, the government must also monitor the production of basic U.S. industries to assure that it does not decline to a point at which national security is threatened. **As in the case of critical materials, the United States should develop a strategy that applies the criteria under existing law to the loss of capacity to produce essential components and materials.**[14] **The President should direct the Departments of Defense and Commerce to identify jointly those components critical to essential production in a military emergency. In addition, the departments should estimate the national security threshold of domestic production for these components.** If U.S. capacity falls below this threshold, the Commerce Department should conduct hearings on the potential threat to national security and should have the authority to recommend action to the President. In order to ensure that defense production benefits from the technological advances and efficiencies engendered by a competitive industrial performance, any proposed action should give preference to stockpiling and avoid recommending import protection of domestic industry.

There should be strict controls on the export of U.S. technology which is truly critical in determining the relative balance of power between East and West. But the system for processing license applications for export approval should be designed for expeditious decisions on whether or not

---

14. The Trade Expansion Act of 1962 (Section 232), Public Law 87-79094 (Washington, D.C.: U.S. Government Printing Office, 1962).

the export will be permitted. If the current system were modernized there is no reason why applications for export to a friendly nation could not be processed within one week.

While it may be useful to restrict a broad range of technological transactions with East Bloc countries, controls on interactions with allies and other trading partners can have counterproductive effects on our economic objectives. The following guidelines are recommended for U.S. exports:*   **

- Export controls are warranted if the export involves truly militarily critical technology, would effectively transfer technological know-how, and the Soviet access to the technology is in fact controllable through regulation.

- For export to allied or other friendly nations who cooperate in a system of controls on such exports, advance approval generally should not be required.

- In trade with free world nations, routine transactions involving commodities and technical information that do not transfer technological know-how should not require advance government approval.

---

*See memorandum by EDMUND B. FITZGERALD, page 139.

**See memorandum by FRANKLIN A. LINDSAY, page 140.

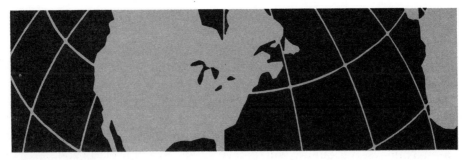

Chapter 4

Facilitating Industrial, Regional, and Labor Market Adjustments

During the 1970s, the U.S. economy, relying on the operation of markets without any direct government planning, produced more than 20 million new jobs and reallocated capital and labor resources to expanding industries and regions. The government plays an important indirect role in helping the market system expand output and employment through macroeconomic policies that encourage growth and productivity improvement. But government microeconomic policies can also improve the operation of markets by facilitating the movement of capital and labor into economic activities in which demand is expanding.

Microeconomic policies to improve markets should be as sector-neutral as possible; that is, they should avoid favoring specific sectors or groups of workers affected by particular types of structural change. The goal of greater neutrality in government intervention does not necessarily justify new intervention. On the contrary, more neutrality in government intervention requires the elimination or major reform of some of the current array of tax, loan, and expenditure policies. At times, special assistance may be necessary to aid specific companies, industries, and regions whose competitiveness is declining. These cases should be treated as exceptions and judged as far as possible on individual merits, including demonstrated efforts to regain competitiveness.

46

TARGETED ASSISTANCE TO FIRMS AND INDUSTRIES

The U.S. government has no explicit targeting policy to make U.S. industries and firms more competitive or to help them adjust to structural economic change. However, like other countries, the United States has an extensive array of expenditures, loans and loan guarantees, and special tax arrangements that assist industry.*

Direct expenditures to support industry represent about 2 percent of annual outlays. Agriculture will receive almost $14 billion in 1984, most of which is to reduce cyclical fluctuations. About $1.8 billion of direct expenditures supports the development of energy-supply technologies. Although there is some targeting of these funds to type of technology, in most cases it is for demonstration projects. There is also some targeting of R and D funds to agriculture, some of which is for nonbasic research and development, but this amounts to less than $1 billion a year and includes distribution of information and marketing assistance to farmers.

Loans and loan guarantees are also used to support industries, with industry receiving about half of the annual net direct loan obligations. Agriculture is also a major beneficiary of this form of assistance.

Special tax preferences are the most important form of assistance to industry when measured by the estimated revenue loss from these features of the corporate tax code. Although few are deliberately targeted to specific industries, some sectors make more use of them than others. It is, of course, highly questionable whether some of the most important tax preferences can legitimately be considered aids to industry. For example, the preferential treatment of capital gains assists industry, but it was introduced partly to offset the excessive taxation of capital gains because no adjustment was made for inflation. Similarly, the accelerated cost recovery system was introduced because employers were unable to write off the full replacement cost of capital under the previous tax treatment of depreciation.

One study found that some sectors received more assistance than others when measured by federal aid as a proportion of industry value added and of new capital investment. Agriculture and, to a lesser extent, mining received more than all other sectors.[1] Manufacturing received slightly more support than trades and services, but if the part of the accelerated capital cost recovery tax treatment designed to reflect the real cost of

1. A major part of the assistance to mining comes from the percentage depletion provision, which can permit firms to write off more than the cost of drilling for oil and gas. This provision is not available to major oil and gas companies.

*See memorandum by PHILIP M. KLUTZNICK, page 141.

capital replacement was *not* counted as assistance to industry, the positions of the two sectors would probably be reversed.[2]

Most government assistance is primarily designed to raise or stabilize income, and is not targeted to make U.S. industries more competitive, as in the case of agriculture. It is not clear how important this has been in making U.S. agriculture one of the most productive sectors of the economy, although it must play an important indirect role. High rates of productivity growth in agriculture may arise primarily from natural resource advantages and from innovation stimulated by incentives for capital investment available to all industries. It is sometimes claimed that by providing farmers with information on innovations developed in universities and by private firms in agribusiness, the government is responsible for much of the success of U.S. agriculture. However, the government resources supporting this diffusion process are relatively small compared with other forms of assistance to farmers.

Industry-specific government assistance is occasionally provided to industries experiencing some type of economic difficulty,[3] but it is generally intended to be temporary or is necessary for social or national security reasons. For example, as in most other countries, the maritime industry receives construction and operating subsidies and benefits from large outstanding loans and loan guarantees. The federal government has sometimes intervened to assist the railroads. Several industries that are subject to unusual cyclical fluctuations, such as dairy, commercial fishing, and forest products, have for many years been the beneficiaries of federal assistance.

Under the Economic Development Administration's (EDA's) Business Development Assistance Program, the textile, apparel, and footwear industries have received loans to modernize plants to help them meet severe import competition. Similarly, EDA is responsible for the Special Steel Loan Program, established in 1978, to provide loans to steel companies to

---

2. Congressional Budget Office, *Federal Support of U.S. Business* (Washington, D.C.: U.S. Congress, 1984), Chapters III and IV.

---

3. The United States has no explicit policy to assist firms in difficulty, but such assistance has occasionally been provided. Under the 1971 Lockheed Guarantee Act, credit guarantees of up to $250 million a year were provided during the 1972-1975 period. Continuing financial difficulties required that the guarantee be extended through 1977, when Lockheed returned to profitability. Under the 1979 Chrysler Corporation Loan Guarantee Act, the company received $1.2 billion but had to obtain $2.0 billion in loans and other concessions from workers, creditors, suppliers, and state and local governments. The loans have now been repaid at less than market rates. See James M. Bickley, *Overviews of the Lockheed, New York City, and Chrysler Loan Guarantee Programs* (Washington, D.C.: Congressional Research Service, U.S. Library of Congress, May 1980).

improve operating efficiency. The magnitude of these subsidies is extremely small compared with the rate of capital investment in each industry.

Adjustment assistance to industries in difficulty sometimes takes the form of temporary import protection to give firms time to introduce new technology or exit from the industry. Examples include trade agreements negotiated with major trading partners, as has been done for textiles. As discussed in Chapter 6, there is now considerable pressure in all major industrial nations to extend these negotiated cartel mechanisms to products such as steel, automobiles, and consumer electronics.

ASSISTING FIRMS AND INDUSTRIES IN ECONOMIC DIFFICULTY

Industries will be able to adjust to structural changes more efficiently if government corrects any bias in existing policies and creates the noninflationary economic environment to encourage long-term investment. In some instances, the government may have political and social reasons for assisting firms or industries experiencing economic difficulties.

In theory, temporary subsidies to improve investment in specific industries can also be justified, but experience has shown that such well-intentioned subsidies frequently inhibit adjustment to structural change. Protection from normal market competition often leads to lower rates of investment and less productivity improvement because the incentive to innovate is lost. Also, a subsidy to one industry or firm usually leads to demands from additional industries and groups of workers for new subsidies or the continuation of existing subsidy programs. Government interventions can also distort market signals, retarding adjustment to change and making the inevitable movement of resources to more promising economic activities more costly.

The current level and growth of government subsidies to industries and companies in the form of expenditures, loans, loan guarantees, tax preferences, and import protection have a detrimental effect on the ability to reduce substantially the federal budget deficit. These subsidies often come to be regarded as a property right by their recipients; and many are, in fact, entitlements under law. Consequently, many programs continue to expand, even though the circumstances that once justified their existence have long since passed.

The current level of subsidies must be reduced on the basis of an evaluation of their purpose and effect on the competitiveness of the economy. In cases where assistance to companies and industries continues to be justified, the subsidies should be countercyclical wherever possible. This means their cost should be less at the peak of an economic recovery and higher during a recession. This feature is desirable because it contributes to the goal of smaller fluctuations in economic activity. This Committee's guidelines for government interventions to reduce the cost of adjustment are summarized in the following paragraphs.

ASSISTANCE TO INDUSTRIES

Consideration should be given to reversing the recent growth of domestic subsidies to specific industries. In estimating the value of such subsidies, the potential benefit to the subsidized industry should be weighed against the cost of opportunities foregone because of the diversion of resources from more promising activities.

Estimating potential benefits and costs is difficult. The benefits of the subsidy are greatest if the industry has a realistic chance of regaining its competitive position and if private capital investment is likely to be attracted to it. The cost will be high if management and labor fail to take the necessary steps to improve productivity and to make the difficult decision to phase out obsolete plant and equipment. The major cost of subsidies is the indirect cost to society of making taxpaying firms in more promising activities finance part of the loss of competitiveness in the subsidized industry.

To ensure that any justifiable subsidy is temporary, it should be accompanied by (1) an explicit assessment of its direct and indirect costs, (2) specific actions to be taken by management and labor, and (3) a prearranged schedule for progressively eliminating the entire subsidy.

ASSISTANCE TO SPECIFIC COMPANIES

As a general principle, where subsidies are justified, they should be directed to the industry rather than to specific companies. Subsidizing individual firms usually reduces competitive forces and causes distortions among suppliers to the industry.[4] In some instances, however, a major employer's loss of competitiveness in a local labor market can impose significant costs on the community. For political and social reasons, the government may feel compelled to subsidize such firms and their employees. These subsidies should be provided on a case-by-case basis. They should be temporary and should be designed to encourage management to improve the efficiency of the local operations and/or should assist in the relocation of workers to other jobs in the local labor market or in areas of expanding employment opportunities. *As this ad hoc temporary assistance is gradually phased out, the ultimate goal in many cases should be to give labor and capital time to move to other economic activities when the operations are terminated.*

---

4. See *Positive Adjustment Policies* (Paris: Organization for Economic Cooperation and Development, 1983), p. 59.

FACILITATING REGIONAL ADJUSTMENT
TO ECONOMIC CHANGE

The need for regional adjustment to change poses a major challenge to government's strategy to improve competitiveness. Economic change will always have regional dimensions, and relative costs of production are constantly changing on the basis of policies initiated by the regions themselves as well as by changes in the value of regional natural resources. Partly for this reason, U.S. policy has for the most part avoided explicit targeting of assistance to regions in economic difficulty. Exceptions might include federal programs for disaster relief, the closing of military bases, defense procurement regulations that give some priority to labor-surplus areas, and the Area Redevelopment Act (ARA) of 1962, which gave some preference to Appalachia. Apart from ARA, the legislative authority for these programs did not designate specific regions for assistance.[5]

All kinds of federal programs, of course, involve differential revenues and expenditures among regions. Many of these policies aim at micro-level effects and are not considered part of a competitiveness strategy because the goal of changes in the federal expenditure pattern is based primarily on the changes in the policy goal of the specific federal program. **Because structural change affects all regions, any federal program to assist areas in economic difficulty should be general rather than targeted to specific regions.**[6]

TAX POLICIES DESIGNED TO DEVELOP LOCAL SECTORS

Some provisions of the personal income tax code also tend to favor specific sectors. For example, owner-occupied housing has been encouraged through the deductibility of mortgage interest and property taxes. This lowers the cost of capital for owner-occupied housing and increases the rate of return from this type of investment. In the past, this certainly stimulated growth in the housing sector, but it also raised the relative cost of capital in other sectors. ERTA substantially reduced this bias by providing some incentives for saving and investment.

---

5. The most publicized exception is the New York City loan guarantee, under which the federal government provided $2.3 billion in short-term loans and, as prescribed in the legislation, the city undertook significant expenditure cuts, budget reforms, and the development of a financial plan that included private lenders.

---

6. For example, displacement due to plant closing is actually larger outside the Northeast and upper Midwest because rapid economic growth inevitably entails greater potential for plant closing. See Candee S. Harris, "Plant Closing: The Magnitude of the Problem," Working Paper no. 13, Business Microdata Project (Washington, D.C.: The Brookings Institution, Photocopy, 1983).

The tax code also permits local jurisdictions to issue bonds with the interest exempt from taxes. Some of these bonds issued by *public* authorities are designed to improve the public infrastructure which may improve the competitiveness of business in local areas.

The tax code also permits states and local authorities or private institutions to issue bonds designed for *private* purposes. In 1975, these private-activity issues accounted for 20 percent of all tax-exempt bonds; they now constitute more than half of the $85 billion issued annually.

Two major disadvantages stem from the rapid growth of tax-exempt issues. First, the overall growth from $30 billion in 1975 to $85 billion in 1981 has distorted the flow of investable funds away from new plant and equipment, which do not receive such favorable tax treatment. The annual volume of investment may have reached the point where it is crowding out some private-sector investment essential to future employment growth.[7] Moreover, the large revenue loss to the U.S. Treasury keeps interest rates high, thereby increasing the difficulty of reducing federal budget deficits.

Second, private-activity issues are growing as a portion of total annual issues. Public issues to improve infrastructure can contribute to a region's economic development, but the same argument does not apply to private-activity issues under the Small Issue Industrial Revenue Bond (SIIRB) program. SIIRBs, which since 1975 have expanded tenfold to a current annual rate of $13.7 billion, have grown more rapidly than other types of bonds.[8] Evaluations of the benefit from this substantial annual loss of federal revenues ($2 to $3 billion) conclude that these bonds make little difference to industrial-location decisions and at best make only a marginal contribution to local employment growth.

The tax-exempt preference given the private-purpose bonds distorts the allocation of capital within local areas. From the point of view of economic development, there is no reason why those issuing the bonds for

---

7. The concern that some private investment is being crowded out is based on the growth of tax-exempt issues as a proportion of personal saving. In 1975 tax-exempt issues were equivalent to 32 percent of personal saving; but by 1981, the proportion had risen to 65 percent. This proportion is, of course, much less when corporate and personal saving are combined. Some of the increase in tax-exempt issues did subsidize business investment for such activities as pollution control, which at least partially offset the crowding-out effect. The policy issues associated with the growth of tax-exempt bonds will be reviewed in a proposed CED project on tax policy.

---

8. Joint Committee on Taxation, *Trends in the Use of Tax-Exempt Bonds to Finance Private Activities, Including A Description of H.R. 1176 and H.R. 1635* (Washington, D.C.: U.S. Government Printing Office, 1983).

52

private purposes should not compete in capital markets on the same basis as those wishing to bring other types of plant and equipment to local areas. Fortunately, policy makers recognize that some reduction in the current level of these state and local issues is required as part of the strategy to reduce projected out-year budget deficits. A reduction in these types of bonds will eliminate some of the distortions caused by the favorable tax treatment given private investment activities through private industrial revenue bonds.

POLICY DIRECTIONS TO FACILITATE REGIONAL ADJUSTMENT TO ECONOMIC CHANGE

In the long run, productive facilities will always tend to move to those regions with the lowest production costs. Unfortunately, labor and, especially public capital, are not always sufficiently mobile to adjust to such structural change. In some cases, the cost of unused public infrastructure imposes substantial costs on communities. On the other hand, when the differences in relative costs of production among regions become pronounced, the short-run political and social cost of dislocation becomes highly visible, but the long-run cost of failure to move resources out of the region is often not fully recognized. Any attempt to offset the immobility of resources out of areas with chronically high unemployment by artificially stimulating economic activity in the area is likely to involve high long-run costs and may have less effect on the area's unemployment rate than anticipated.

The federal government funds several major economic development programs.[9] For most programs the federal government plays the major role in determining which industries and firms are to receive assistance. Information on how such programs are likely to affect the revitalization of local industries is most readily available at the local area. Since actions for restoring the competitiveness of local economies depend heavily on local public policies, as well as actions taken by local management and labor, the decision on how to integrate current programs for federal assistance with local revitalization efforts should be made as close as possible to the local level. **Serious consideration should be given to merging several**

---

9. For an evaluation of the sectoral effect of selected credit programs see Nonno A. Noto, *Industrial Policy Implicit in Federal Business Credit Programs* (Washington, D.C.: Congressional Research Service, U.S. Library of Congress, December 1980).

**existing programs within a block grant for economic development that
would be distributed to state and local authorities on the basis of a stated
formula.**[10] This merging would also provide an opportunity to reduce
unnecessary overlap among federal programs and avoid waste of resources
by reducing the cost of this assistance.

The criteria used in the distribution formula may include the trends in
income and long-term unemployment, with local authorities deciding how
economic development block grants would be utilized. In the longer run,
the economic development of a region will be more rapid if the local
government takes steps to reduce the area's cost disadvantage, including a
reduction in general business taxes and improvement of public infrastructure.

LABOR MARKET ADJUSTMENTS TO STRUCTURAL CHANGE

Studies of the effect of technological change and the potential applications of innovations in many industries conclude that this form of structural
change will displace some workers from their current jobs but that the net
effect will be to stimulate employment throughout the economy.[11] The
government's prime role should be to facilitate readjustment of workers
who are *permanently* dislocated from their previous jobs and to avoid skill
shortages in growing occupations.

High unemployment and the growing awareness of the need to introduce new technology to increase competitiveness have given rise to fears
that unemployment because of structural changes in the economy will
become more rapid and lead to greater skill obsolescence in the future.
There is no evidence that future structural change will be so rapid that it will
cause large-scale permanent labor force dislocation or that there will be a
need to retrain a substantial proportion of the work force (see box page 54).
Similarly, although no skill shortages are currently predicted, these official

---

10. The economic development-programs that might be merged should probably include the Urban
Development Action Grants and the Community Development Block Grants as well as EDA's Business
Development Assistance Programs, the Small Business Administration's regular business loan program
and the Farmer's Home Administration's Business Development Assistance Program.

---

11. See Robert Ayers and Steve Miller, *The Impact of Industrial Robots* (Pittsburgh: The Robotics
Institute, Carnegie-Mellon University, 1982) and Robert A. Levy, Marianne Bowers, James M. Jondrow,
"Technical Change and Employment in Five Industries: Steel, Autos, Aluminum, Coal and Iron Ore," in
Eileen L. Collins and Lucretia Dewey-Tanner, eds., *American Jobs and the Changing Industrial Base*
(Boston, Mass.: Ballinger, forthcoming 1984).

estimates may prove inaccurate. In the long run, the quality of education, especially at the precollege level, will determine the ability of the nation's labor force to adapt to change. There is considerable evidence that *unless the educational system improves the basic educational skills (such as mathematics, science, English, and computer operation) of all students, the labor force will become less adaptable to change.* * [12]

The future growth of manufacturing employment depends heavily on the rate of capital investment. The government estimates that in the short run, manufacturing employment will continue to increase but will constitute a declining share of the labor force through 1990. At the same time,

---

12. A forthcoming CED policy statement will examine the role of business in education.

STRUCTURAL CHANGE WILL GRADUALLY ALTER THE COMPOSITION OF THE LABOR FORCE AND THE DEMAND FOR LABOR SKILLS

- During the 1980s, the growth rate of employment in most services will moderate to between 2 and 3 percent a year. By 1990, it is expected that business and personal services will account for about 22 percent of the labor force.

- During the same period, the number of manufacturing jobs will expand at less than 1 percent a year, but the proportion of jobs in this sector will decline slightly to about 19.4 percent of the labor force by the end of the decade.[a]

Evaluations of shortages in occupations such as machinists and engineers confirm that shortages existed in the past, but only in some of the more specific occupations within these broader occupational categories.

- During the 1970s, industry appears to have experienced a shortage of highly skilled machinists (e.g., tool and die setters and makers), but not in the many categories within the operative machining group of occupations.

- Employers did not appear to respond to the shortage by raising the relative wage rates of workers with shortage skills. The response was to increase additions to apprenticeship programs.[b]

---

*See memorandum by CLIFTON R. WHARTON, Jr., page 141.

there will be a substantial shift in employment among firms *within* the manufacturing sector. In companies and industries that invest rapidly in new plant and equipment or phase out obsolete plants quickly, workers will face a greater risk of structural unemployment. Similarly, if public policies are successful in raising U.S. productivity growth rates through higher rates of capital investment, the pace of structural change will gradually increase during the next decade.

The high unemployment rate of 1982 was largely attributable to the 1981-1982 recession, and most out of work now have not been laid off because of changes in the structure of the economy. Plant closings, firms going out of business, and the establishment of new enterprises are dynamic processes within the U.S. economy. Plant closings are more common in areas

- During the latter part of the 1970s, the National Science Foundation (NSF) reported that industry was experiencing shortages in several occupations within the broad engineering category. However, by the early 1980s, the NSF concluded that the supply of engineers in all occupations had risen to meet the demand.

The inevitability of future shortages in engineering and machine tool skill categories is not confirmed by empirical data.

- The alleged aging of America's machinists is simply not occurring. Between 1972 and 1980, the proportion of these workers aged 55 to 64 declined, and significant increases in the proportion of these workers in the 20-to-25 and 25-to-34 age groups were recorded.[c]

- The future applications of numerical control technology in manufacturing are likely to reduce the growth in demand for highly skilled machinists and offset any shortage that existed in the 1970s.

- According to the NSF, significant increases in college enrollment in engineering will substantially increase the supply of engineers to meet industry's needs, even with an increase in defense expenditures. However, unless academic institutions respond to shortages of faculty in some engineering fields, the current faculty shortage may continue into the 1980s, and this might reduce the growth of undergraduate engineers.

a. See Valeria A. Personick, "The Outlook for Industry Output and Employment through 1990," *Monthly Labor Review* 104, No. 8 (August 1981), pp. 24-41.

b. See Neal H. Rosenthal, "Shortages of Machinists: An Evaluation of the Information," *Monthly Labor Review* (July 1982), pp. 31-36.

c. Rosenthal, "Shortages of Machinists: An Evaluation of the Information," p. 35.

56

of rapid business formation, such as the South and Pacific regions, than in the Northeast and upper Midwest.[13] But the reemployment of workers displaced by changes in net business formation is also more rapid in regions of dynamic economic growth, and only a small proportion of those who lose their jobs through plant closings in expanding areas are likely to be unemployed for a long period of time. On the other hand, in communities where the traditional industrial base is concentrated, the closing of a major manufacturing plant can create substantial difficulties for the reemployment of the local labor force.

To distinguish between those who are unemployed for cyclical reasons and those who lose their jobs because of changes in technology, trade, and consumer preferences, considerations other than "loss of job" should be taken into account. For example, one approach argues that the permanently displaced worker must not only be laid off without recall but must also experience long-term unemployment of perhaps twenty-six weeks or more. In some estimates, the worker must be laid off in an area or an industry with declining employment.[14] Consequently, estimates of the number of displaced workers range from about 100,000 to over 1 million per year. For the 1981-1982 recession, data on job losers experiencing long-term unemployment suggest that 5 to 10 percent of the unemployed were laid off for structural reasons.[15]

Although displacement occurs in all industries, it is most visible within the traditional U.S. industrial base. Many of these industries are characterized by a small number of firms, but the scale of operations is typically large, so that a plant closing can have a significant impact in a local labor market. In industries such as autos and steel, reemployment after a plant

---

13. See Candee S. Harris, "Plant Closing: The Magnitude of the Problem."

---

14. See Congressional Budget Office, "Dislocated Workers: Issues and Federal Options" (Washington, D.C.: Congressional Budget Office, 1982).

---

15. See U.S. Department of Labor, Bureau of Labor Statistics, *Current Population Survey*. According to the Bureau of Labor Statistics, there were about 2.8 million job losers in 1981, of whom about 600,000 (21 percent) experienced twenty-seven or more weeks of unemployment. Because most of these workers were laid off due to plant closing and permanent reductions in the work force, with no indication that they would be recalled, 600,000 represents an approximate estimate of the structural component of those who were unemployed during the year. In 1982, almost 4.2 million workers lost their jobs without recall, and about 1 million (23.6 percent) experienced twenty-seven weeks or more of unemployment. In previous recessions, even severe ones, about 80 percent of job losers eventually returned to the same employer. If it is assumed that the 1981-1982 recession had a larger structural component than previous recessions and that only 70 percent of job losers can expect to return eventually to their previous employment, the estimate is in the 600,000-to-1,000,000 range for the annual number of those structurally unemployed during an extremely severe recession.

closing is even more difficult because those laid off are experienced workers whose wage rates have risen well above the average for other manufacturing workers. Many displaced workers in these industries will experience permanent earnings losses as they are eventually forced to relocate in jobs with lower wage rates.

Much of the adjustment to increased structural change can be accomplished through attrition as workers retire. In addition, the United States has always had the advantage of a highly mobile work force. For example, during the 1979-1980 period, some 50 percent of those separated from their jobs were reemployed in a *different* occupation within a year.[16] Consequently, if the pace of structural change increases in many basic industries, much of the adjustment will occur automatically as displaced workers move to the growth occupations, especially in related industries and occupations.

This flexibility contrasts sharply with lack of labor mobility in other countries. Many other industrial countries, in response to the 1976 worldwide recession, adopted policies that increased labor market rigidities in an attempt to protect jobs. This probably contributed to the much slower employment growth and subsequently to the much higher rate of structural unemployment in a number of industrial countries than in the United States. Although most U.S. labor markets are reasonably effective in relocating workers, the actions of management and labor as well as the government can do much to facilitate the movement of displaced workers to new employment opportunities and reduce the adjustment costs.

PRIVATE-SECTOR POLICIES TO ASSIST PERMANENTLY DISPLACED WORKERS

Management's personnel policies and practices can help permanently displaced workers adjust to change. In collective bargaining situations, management and labor have frequently negotiated agreements providing workers with severance rights; in others, they have organized a system of retraining for workers in which local public education and training institutions have participated.

CHANGING THE LEVEL AND STRUCTURE OF EMPLOYEE COMPENSATION. Personnel policies, as well as labor-management negotiations concerning relative compensation structures can do much to moderate the pace of structural change as well as ease the transition for dislocated workers. Because loss of competitiveness changes the demand for labor,

---

16. Based on unpublished data supplied by the U.S. Department of Labor, Bureau of Labor Statistics.

flexibility in employee compensation is critical to the amount of adjustment necessary.

The concept of total compensation flexibility cannot be a euphemism for reducing workers' share of economic growth through a general cutback in wages and benefits. Nor can compensation inflexibility be charged as the sole cause of loss of competitiveness. But in competitive markets total compensation costs must reflect the condition of the enterprise and its stage of development.

Young, productive enterprises are constantly emerging as new businesses, or as new activities spawned by existing firms. The compensation package of these businesses is initially characterized by relatively lower wage and benefit structures. If successful, these enterprises become part of the economic mainstream and jobs, wages, and benefits expand together.

On the basis of past growth, many firms in industries that have reached a stable mature stage have relatively high compensation costs. If subjected to competition from newer businesses with more modern equipment, lower-paid work forces, or lower unit costs of production, the economic viability of the older enterprise will be threatened. Compensation flexibility is one of the ways which can help the more mature firm retain its vitality and respond to the competitive threat. If the mature firm fails to innovate and continues the habit of percentage wage growth and benefit improvement its vulnerability increases. In this case compensation inflexibility contributes to the loss of employment resulting from failure to adjust to the new competitive environment.

During the past decade, the government has indirectly played a role in increasing compensation inflexibility through the growth of legislated benefits. But management and labor have been slow to recognize the advantage of designing a compensation package that rewards employees for contributing to the innovation so necessary for retaining the vitality of the enterprise.[17]

Moderating growth in employee compensation can do much to improve the competitive position of firms and reduce the threat to the employment security of workers. But employees in some industries will have to take an absolute decline in real compensation because their compensation increases during the 1970s were clearly out of line with productivity improvement and competitive labor market wage rates. In some instances, management and labor have agreed to real reductions in response to loss of the firm's market share. In the short run, this is a highly desirable response to

---

17. For a further discussion of this issue see Doyle and McLennan, "Employment Growth in the Context of Structural Change."

economic change. The decline in the rate of inflation and the 1981-1982 recession resulted in a significant reduction in the annual percentage increase in wages.[18] This will also increase the prospects for labor market adjustment through future employment growth. In the long run, however, successful adjustment will be achieved only through greater productivity brought about by innovation within the firm. *The greatest threat to employment security comes from failure to innovate. Unless a company becomes more productive, it is inevitable that some of the work force will become permanently displaced and may experience permanent income losses through long-term unemployment and the eventual need to accept lower-paying jobs.*

It is true that some innovation can result in worker dislocation, but the magnitude of this problem is relatively small because the introduction and diffusion of innovation in industry is usually a gradual process. This makes it easier to reduce the extent of job loss through normal attrition of the work force. Downward adjustment of compensation levels and/or growth rates can mitigate the extent of worker displacement and is therefore an essential component of labor market adjustment; but it is only a partial solution.

ADJUSTMENT ASSISTANCE IN RESPONSE TO PLANT CLOSINGS. Current legislative proposals for specific actions in the case of plant closings and major reductions in the work force would be counterproductive. Experience in Europe suggests that mandatory prenotification and severance programs have not facilitated readjustment. The stereotype of the permanently displaced worker is someone laid off from a large firm in the basic manufacturing sector, but this is inaccurate. In reality, plant closings are more common among smaller firms located outside the traditional manufacturing areas of the Northeast and upper Midwest. For most firms that close plants, it would be impossible to design and enforce legislation. Many larger companies would also have difficulty providing prenotification of plant closing because in some industries the failure to secure a major contract (e.g., a defense contract) can lead to an immediate cessation of operations that quickly affects a network of supplier firms.

Nevertheless, many employers are in a position to develop voluntarily personnel policies to ease the transition of workers laid off when the plant is closed. Because these policies are likely to vary by industry and by size, and financial resources of the firm, it is much more effective if management,

---

18. During the 1976-1981 period, the hourly earnings index for all industries rose at an average annual rate of 8.2 percent. The index peaked at 9.2 percent in 1980 and dropped to 3.6 percent in 1983. Data updated from Wayne Vroman, *Wage Inflation* (Washington, D.C.: The Urban Institute, 1983), pp. 8-9.

60

preferably with union and/or worker participation, adopts voluntary guidelines for actions to assist those who are permanently displaced. In some firms and industries subject to rapid fluctuations in output, the emphasis will be on severance payments; for companies with a more predictable demand, more advanced planning and notification will be more effective.

Several industry groups have developed voluntary guidelines for plant closings. The Business Roundtable (BRT) has drawn up an imaginative set that includes options of prenotification, severance pay, extension of benefit coverage, and cooperation with public-sector training and relocation programs.[19] **We endorse this voluntary approach because it provides for the cooperation of those directly involved; it encourages resolution of some of the adjustment problems by those who have the greatest incentive to minimize the economic and social disruptions, and can be based on the particular facts of each case.**

GOVERNMENT POLICIES TO ASSIST
DISLOCATED WORKERS

Existing federal worker-adjustment programs, many of which were designed to assist specific groups, have generally proved ineffective in facilitating adjustment. The rationale for those programs was that other government actions such as deregulation of an industry, expansion of a national park, a modification of federal health care policy, or a reduction in tariff barriers indirectly hurt an industry. But experience both here and abroad has shown that well-intentioned public policies to encourage adjustment to economic change frequently end up protecting existing jobs and the income of a relatively small group of workers while failing to encourage these workers to move to more productive employment.[20] Ideally, it would be de-

19. *BRT Position Paper on Plant Closings* (Washington, D.C.: The Business Roundtable, Mimeographed, 1983). See also National Association of Manufacturers, *When a Plant Closes: A Guide to Employers* (Washington, D.C.: National Association of Manufacturers, 1983).

20. The United States currently has about twenty adjustment assistance programs targeted on specific groups of displaced workers, such as hospital employees, federal government workers, and those affected by changes in government policies. Many of these well-intentioned adjustment programs actually discouraged workers from moving to other employment opportunities, even though retraining and relocation was available to those laid off. The Trade Adjustment Assistance program under the 1974 Trade Act was the largest of such programs and proved to be particularly ineffective in encouraging adjustment. Over 70 percent of those in the program returned to their previous employer. Only 1.2 percent of laid-off workers took advantage of the retraining opportunity; 0.3 percent took advantage of the relocation allowances. This program has recently been reauthorized with a number of reforms designed to reduce the incentive for workers to rely on the income maintenance feature of the program and wait to be rehired.

sirable if these targeted programs were phased out as the government improved general adjustment programs.

During a period of structural change, the government can play a role in retraining and relocating permanently displaced employees. For example, the limited funds available under Title III of the Job Partnership Training Act may help train experienced workers who have been permanently dislocated. CED strongly endorses the feature of the act which requires that the type of training and the delivery of the training services be made at the local level because local labor, business, and public institutions are in the best position to assist displaced workers.

It is inconsistent with the concern about the federal budget deficit to advocate an increase in government expenditures for existing targeted assistance programs or new training programs for assisting displaced workers. There are already considerable resources available in the government's general programs to encourage education and in the unemployment insurance (UI) program, which involves annual outlays of between $15 and $30 billion, depending on the rate of unemployment. The most appropriate strategy is to improve the *flexibility* of these programs so that displaced workers can use them to improve their labor market opportunities.[21]

IMPROVING THE FLEXIBILITY OF EDUCATIONAL ASSISTANCE

Some displaced workers may benefit from job-related training provided by the vocational education system. Current regulations make it difficult for displaced workers to qualify for a student grant or loan that could be used as income while receiving retraining. The following policy changes could make these programs more accessible to displaced workers:

- The principal place of residence of a displaced worker who has been unemployed for twenty-six weeks would not be counted in the asset test for a student loan or grant. Similarly, the receipt of extended UI benefits would not be counted toward meeting the income test.

---

21. For an assessment of the Unemployment Insurance system's role in assisting displaced workers, see Kenneth McLennan, "Unemployment Insurance: To Help Dislocated Workers," *The Journal of the Institute of Socioeconomic Studies,* (New York: Volume VIII, Number 2, 1983) pp.59-73. For a detailed review of the policy options to assist displaced workers, see Kenneth McLennan, "Policy Options to Facilitate the Reemployment of Displaced Workers," in *The Displaced Worker Problem: Implications for Training and Education Institutions,* eds., Kevin Hollenbeck, Frank Pratzner, and Howard Rosen (Columbus, Ohio: National Center for Research in Vocational Education, The Ohio State University, forthcoming 1984), Chapter 18. Also, see Stephen E. Baldwin and Anne Donohue, "Displaced Workers: New Options for a Changing Economy" (Washington, D.C.: National Commission for Employment Policy, Mimeographed, 1983).

- For displaced workers, the *"full-time student" regulation could be waived* so that displaced workers could receive educational assistance even though they are enrolled only in a part-time training course. This modification could be important in those states whose UI program permits workers to earn some income and still be eligible for UI benefits.

IMPROVING THE EFFICIENCY OF THE UI SYSTEM

Many state UI funds are now in serious deficit, and many will continue in a weak financial position through the end of the decade. Therefore, any policy changes to increase the resources available to help permanently displaced workers adjust to structural change must be offset by a reduction in inefficient use of resources for overpayments, which independent reviews of UI claims indicate probably amount to between 10 and 20 percent of benefits, depending on the city or state.[22]

Although many state UI systems will find it necessary to increase the employer UI wage tax, the recent trend toward financing social policies through increases in wage taxes (as in the case of Social Security) is already raising the cost of hiring. In 1976, additional compensation for manufacturing workers was about 31 percent of hourly earnings; by 1982, this had increased to 39 percent. Government mandated wage costs now amount to about 8.3 percent of wages and are projected to rise over the next several years as Social Security tax increases are introduced. This trend can only increase the difficulty of facilitating labor market readjustment through employment growth. Proposals to finance worker training accounts through an increase in hiring costs would be counterproductive. Every effort must be made to improve the efficiency of the UI system and avoid unnecessary increases in hiring costs through a further round of wage tax increases.

We suggest that the following UI policy changes be considered as ways to improve the efficiency of the UI system:

---

22. This estimate is based on the results of detailed research of the administration of the UI system in several cities. See Paul L. Burgess and Jerry L. Kingston, "Estimating Overpayments and Improper Payments," in National Commission on Unemployment Compensation, *Unemployment Compensation: Studies and Research*, Vol. 2 (Washington, D.C.: U.S. Government Printing Office, 1980), pp. 487-526. The U.S. Department of Labor funded a project to estimate overpayment in five states during the 1981-1982 period when the unemployment rate was high. Overpayments, as a percent of UI benefits paid statewide, were found to vary from 7.3 to 24.3 percent and averaged 14.2 percent for the five states combined. Underpayments were less than 1 percent of benefits paid in all states. See Paul L. Burgess, Jerry L. Kingston and Robert D. St. Louis, *The Development of an Operational System for Detecting UI Payment Errors Through Random Audits: The Results of Five Statewide Pilot Tests* (Washington, D.C.: Unemployment Insurance Service, U.S. Department of Labor, 1982). See also Comptroller General, *Unemployment Insurance — Need to Reduce Unequal Treatment of Claimants and Improve Benefit Payment Controls and Tax Collection* (Washington, D.C.: U.S. General Accounting Office, April 5, 1978).

- Eleven states now have no waiting period for benefits. This encourages overuse of the system, and no attempt is made to help those unemployed assess whether they are permanently displaced. One approach to reducing this inefficient use of UI resources might be to require states to have *a minimum waiting period of ten days or two weeks before the basic program starts paying benefits for up to twenty-six weeks.*

- The efficiency of labor markets may be improved if the unemployed worker was required to register for a UI-administered *job-search seminar* during the mandatory waiting period. This would help the worker to make a realistic assessment of future employment opportunities and provide him or her with training in how to find alternative employment opportunities in the local labor market.

- Over the years, the proportion of benefits subject to the experience-rated tax has declined substantially. In some states, only 50 percent of benefits paid are now based on the employer's experience in the use of the system. There is, of course, a case for some spreading of the cost to assist firms in cyclically sensitive industries. However, if all states had a tax structure which over a period of years ensured that 70 to 80 percent of benefits were experience-rated, it would improve the incentive for efficient management of human resources and at the same time recognize the unique problem of firms that continue to experience large cyclical fluctuations in demand.

  Consistent with the proposal to encourage management to plan for structural change and use labor resources efficiently, we suggest strengthening experience rating through gradually changing the UI tax structure. All states have some form of experience rating, in which the employer tax is related to the number of employees who draw benefits out of the state system. The larger the differential between the maximum and minimum UI tax rates, the greater the incentive for the employer to utilize the work force efficiently, including maintaining a more stable level of employment.

INCREASING THE FLEXIBILITY OF THE UI SYSTEM

The goal of the UI system should be to give all workers, especially those experiencing long-term unemployment, an incentive to seek employment and return to work as soon as possible. At present, there is little incentive in the benefit structure to encourage the unemployed worker to improve his or her skills or seek alternative employment. We recommend that the following option be considered as part of a strategy to move displaced workers to more productive activities.

- Federal and state unemployment insurance laws do not prohibit unemployed workers from receiving UI benefits when enrolled in an "approved" retraining program. In the past, however, under the administration of the UI program, in most states, few retraining programs have been "approved." *This discourages training.* Some unemployed workers may feel that additional training will equip them for expanding job opportunities. Perhaps the unemployed worker could be eligible to receive training and UI benefits simultaneously after about eight weeks of unemployment. By that time, it should be possible for the worker to determine whether he or she is likely to be displaced permanently or is experiencing cyclical unemployment. Fortunately, an increasing number of states are now beginning to move toward more liberal approval of training programs and the federal government has made it mandatory that displaced workers enrolled in training programs under Title III of the Job Training Partnership Act cannot be denied UI benefits.

Regular UI benefits end after twenty-six weeks, and unemployed workers in states with high unemployment become eligible for federal extended benefits, which continue for thirteen weeks. The labor market would be much more efficient if these extended benefits "triggered on" when the unemployment rate was high in the local labor market rather than when the state average unemployment rate was high.

- *Extended unemployment benefits should be available only when the local labor market rate of unemployment is high.* There are many local labor markets with very low unemployment rates even though the state's average unemployment is sufficiently high to trigger the extended benefits. Almost all states could be divided into a number of labor markets that would be used to determine the availability of extended benefits.

More flexible use of extended benefits should also be considered. These benefits should provide the worker with a strong incentive to find alternative employment.

- One approach would be to *reduce gradually the weekly benefit level* throughout the extended-benefit period.
- An alternative approach is to permit the worker to use extended benefits as a *reemployment voucher.*

— Under the reemployment voucher system, the cost of hiring a permanently dislocated worker (and other long-term-unemployed workers) would be reduced by permitting the worker to convert extended UI benefits into a reemployment voucher to be paid to his or her new employer.

— The value of the voucher could equal 75 percent of the value of the thirteen weeks under the federal extended-benefit program or any remaining weeks for which workers would be eligible if they remained unemployed during the entire extended period. This voucher could be offered to an employer who provides the worker with a job that represents an incremental increase in the employer's work force. The employer would receive the value of the reemployment voucher in quarterly payments from the state UI system or as an offset against quarterly tax payments to the federal government. The incremental wage subsidy through the reemployment voucher would end once the extended-benefit program automatically terminates as the unemployment rate declines.

Serious consideration should also be given to reforming the regular UI program to provide a strong incentive for the displaced older worker to move quickly to another available job when it is clear that permanent displacement has occurred.

- This might take the form of a *work incentive compensation* that would provide a temporary phased-in payment chargeable under the current UI system to the old employer and paid in lieu of regular UI benefits for a fixed period of time following reemployment in a lower paying job.

  For example, the work incentive payment could make up 90 percent of the difference between the old, higher paid rate and the new, lower paid rate for the first two months of employment at the new rate. The differential could be reduced gradually over the next four months to a final 50 percent make-up. The initial weekly work incentive payment would be limited to not more than the 1.25 times the individual's weekly benefit amount and would be payable for no longer than 26 weeks, including any period during which regular UI benefits were paid. The object would be to provide the needed incentive for the displaced employee to accept available employment in an initially lower paying but growing industry and at the same time to reduce the employer's UI benefit costs.

By limiting this option to older permanently displaced workers it will provide an incentive for such workers to move quickly from their former high-paying jobs to lower paying jobs in other occupations or industries. After the period when the worker receives the wage subsidy and on-the-job experience it is likely to be especially helpful for those displaced in local areas in which employment is dependent on the economic position of a major employer.

Provided the UI system is reformed to reduce substantially the level of overpayments and increase the overall efficiency of the system, it may be possible to consider adding a second tier to the current program in the form of an individual account.*

- Tier I would be a modified version of the present system with more effective experience rating and a longer waiting period. Tier II, the individual account, would be financed by a portion (perhaps 10 percent) of the employer tax. Each account should be fully funded. Interest should accrue to the individual account through investment in U.S. Treasury bills.

The eligibility conditions under which a worker could draw upon the account might include: (1) permanent displacement, perhaps with the employer certifying that the worker will not be rehired because the job has been permanently eliminated, or twenty-six weeks of unemployment and (2) continuous labor force experience of five years prior to permanent layoff.

For the average employer, the 10 percent contribution would be offset by the cost savings achieved through improved experience rating and the longer mandatory minimum waiting period. The funds in the individual account would accumulate with work experience and would be available for those who are likely to have the greatest difficulty in adjusting to structural change (e.g., workers with a substantial work history).

It is important to permit the worker to have control over how the funds in the individual account are utilized once he or she is eligible to draw on the account. The amount of withdrawal and whether it is taken in the form of income maintenance, retraining, or relocation should be the worker's decision.

To provide the maximum incentive for the worker to readjust quickly after permanent displacement, it is probably desirable for a small por-

---

*See memorandum by THEODORE A. BURTIS, page 142.

tion of the accrued balance in the account plus interest to go to the worker upon retirement. The remainder would be returned to the state UI fund.

There is clearly a need to experiment with the UI system and with the substantial resources already available for formal education and retraining. In the future, UI benefits should continue to assist workers' search for jobs as well as provide important countercyclical income maintenance. However, during 1983, the cost of unemployed workers, both to their families and to society, was high. The issue is whether we can design a more efficient UI system by reducing inherent overpayments and work disincentives while allocating more of the resources to those who really need reemployment assistance.

Chapter 5

The Role of Regulatory and Antitrust Policies in a Competitive Strategy

A competitive strategy that relies primarily upon market forces must assure that private actions do not interfere with markets' ability to function. It also must recognize that markets cannot be counted upon to attain all important social goals. Traditionally, we have turned to regulation when we believed that markets could not be made to function appropriately, and antitrust policy has been a significant component of this regulation.

As the United States has found itself increasingly competing in the world economy, a number of questions have arisen. For example, is the regulation of important infrastructure industries such as transportation, telecommunications, banking, and power generation and transmission still required? Where we must regulate, can we do it in ways that are less costly, intrusive, and inflexible than the present mandated regulatory instruments and at the same time achieve stated regulatory goals? Are current antitrust policy and regulatory policies still appropriate? Does antitrust policy retain a useful role in our modern, complex, internationalized economy?

In examining some recent shifts in views on regulatory and antitrust policies and asking whether further changes are necessary to meet the needs of a strategy to improve U.S. competitiveness, we draw heavily on previous CED policy statements that have addressed certain aspects of this subject.

REASSESSING REGULATION'S ROLE

The past decade or so has seen two seemingly conflicting trends in regulation. The first has been the scaling back and, in some cases, even the total elimination of the regulatory apparatus by which prices, entry and exit, and conditions of service have been controlled in industries such as intercity transportation, telecommunications, and financial services. The second has been the vast expansion of regulation aimed at achieving broad social goals such as the control of environmental pollution, the assurance of safe and healthy working conditions, the safety of consumer products, and equal employment opportunity.

The conflict in these two trends is more apparent than real. The contracting of economic regulation has been spurred by the realization that the original goals that economic regulation sought to achieve were either unattainable or no longer desirable and that the market was generally capable of assuring that the services in question were adequately available and fairly priced. The expansion of social or protective regulation has been stimulated, at least in part, by the realization that markets cannot always be counted on to achieve social goals.

The elimination of economic regulation has enjoyed broad bipartisan support. But precisely how far it will eventually extend is unclear, and in general, the issue is more one of degree than of principle. Within a few years, most of the industries that were once subject to strict economic regulation will face no more restrictions on their operations than other businesses.

In sharp contrast, some features of some types of social regulation have continued to be highly controversial. The benefits hoped for by its proponents have not always been realized. The costs of much social regulation have been massive, and their intrusiveness has been great. Some would argue that social regulation's unimpressive performance stems principally from a lack of zeal on the part of those who have administered it and from the outright hostility of business toward its goals. Others, including its supporters, candidly admit that the original hopes were unrealistic, that the techniques of regulation employed have virtually assured that the goals would not be attained, and that whatever progress we have made has been at an unnecessarily high cost.

In general, reform of social regulation has not meant eliminating specific regulatory programs. Rather, it has focused on administering them in a more cost-effective and flexible manner, with increased attention given to competing social goals and to the possible trade-offs between these goals and the benefits of economic growth.

To reform social regulation, it is necessary to create a political climate in which there is consensus that the broad goals of the regulations are desirable. Without this consensus, reforming the implementation through market-based incentives becomes extremely difficult. The current absence of consensus in the business community over some social regulations has translated the debate about social regulation's means into a debate about its goals. In the process, progress toward improving the means of achieving some social regulatory goals efficiently has been sidetracked.

In previous policy statements,[1] CED has emphasized that although continuing efforts at social regulation are clearly justified, the programs now on the books are very much in need of major reform. We have outlined the direction we believe this reform should take: a better balancing of regulation's benefits against its costs; the use of less costly, less intrusive regulatory techniques; and a more realistic sense of the fact that many government solutions fail to improve significantly upon those produced by admittedly imperfect markets. A summary of these recommendations is presented in "CED's Approach to Determining and Achieving Regulatory Goals" (pages 72-73).

What concerns us now is *how* the reforms we have previously recommended can be brought to pass. Objections to the sort of recommendations that CED has made run deep and are not easily overcome. Surveys have shown that even individuals who understand the efficiency implications of innovative regulatory techniques often view efforts to implement them with extreme suspicion, considering such efforts as disguised attempts to gut the programs they support. Resistance also comes from many in the business community who, for all their complaints about overregulation, have learned to live with the current system and fear change.

Social regulatory programs have to be well designed to achieve realistic regulatory goals efficiently. While such programs do not have to be administered by technicians, those responsible for regulatory management must be knowledgeable about the programs and capable of integrating program evaluations into regulatory policies. The administration of such programs should be funded at levels commensurate with achieving regulatory goals.

The determination and implementation of regulatory goals are important political decisions that inevitably give rise to differences of opinion on the trade-off between the desirability of a particular goal and the benefits foregone by diverting resources to achieve it. Efforts to introduce flexibility

---

1. See *Productivity Policy: Key to the Nation's Economic Future* and *Redefining Government's Role in the Market System.*

into enforcement must therefore be seen as enhancing program effectiveness, and the results of cost-benefit studies of regulation cannot be selectively employed to block the implementation of regulations. Nor conversely should the argument that cost-benefit studies are not precise preclude a critical review of regulatory programs.

Regulatory policy is a dynamic process. How to achieve widely supported regulatory programs should be part of a systematic regulatory review so that desirable policies can be efficiently implemented. But the goals of specific regulatory programs are also subject to change. On the basis of experience, if a regulatory policy is judged by policy makers to be unrealistic or undesirable, the political process will either eliminate the policy or redefine its original goal. Similarly, in the political process, some goals may be viewed as not sufficiently stringent, and new standards for industry will need to be established. The CED approach to determining and achieving regulatory goals to enhance competitiveness in U.S. industry and at the same time meet desirable social goals implies that policy changes should be based as much as possible on an evaluation of costs and benefits within the political process.

Much regulation can and should be eliminated. But regulation will remain an important element in our economy's competitiveness. However, necessary regulation must be conducted in a manner that does not generate unnecessary burdens on the economy or create unnecessary uncertainties about future implementation. The nation has enough resources to achieve important social goals. It does not have enough to be indifferent about *how* it achieves them.

ANTITRUST POLICY: HAS REFORM GONE FAR ENOUGH?

For nearly a century, the United States has had an extensive regulatory system prohibiting certain monopolies, restraints of trade, and conspiracies. Over the years, antitrust zeal and enforcement have varied in intensity. Only a decade ago, Congress was seriously debating legislation making the mere *possession* of a given market share an offense under the antitrust law, even though the market was relatively competitive. In the late 1960s and early 1970s, the Antitrust Division of the Department of Justice brought a number of cases against large firms holding significant market positions. In 1969, a suit was filed against IBM; AT&T was sued in 1974. In recent years, however, the situation has moderated considerably, with few policy makers asserting that attainment of a specific market share is automatically an antitrust offense. Concern about the anticompetitive effects of mergers has also declined, though it by no means has disappeared. Efforts to apply merger

CED'S APPROACH TO DETERMINING AND ACHIEVING REGULATORY GOALS[a]

DETERMINING WHETHER REGULATION IS JUSTIFIED

- What is the policy's objective and how is it related to a market limitation?

- Will the policy increase competition by eliminating restrictions on entry, improving information, or eliminating restraints on the price mechanism?

- Is government action required because the market is producing some undesirable side effects such as pollution?

- What impact will this have on other overall economic objectives such as improved technological innovation, satisfactory economic growth, reducing the rate of inflation, and achieving high employment?

- What is the impact of international competitiveness on U.S. industries?

- What social and/or political goal is the government seeking?
    — What is the policy's objective?
    — In what manner will the beneficiaries gain?
    — Which citizens will bear the cost?
    — What impact will this have on other overall economic objectives?
    — Is government's goal feasible?
    — Could the stated goal of the proposed government involvement be achieved more efficiently by eliminating an existing government involvement?
    — Is the regulation likely to produce a result that is superior to an imperfectly functioning market?

- What are the proposal's side effects, and what will they cost?

- How do the costs and hoped-for benefits compare?

IMPLEMENTING JUSTIFIABLE REGULATORY INTERVENTIONS

- When policy makers want to achieve performance goals, they should try to devise incentives and penalties, rather than dictate one path that industry must follow in order to comply.

- Whenever it is absolutely necessary for government to establish detailed goals for institutions and individuals to achieve within the economic system, government should avoid prescribing how these goals should be met.

- In establishing performance goals, it should be recognized that attempting to achieve zero-risk standards wastes resources which could be used to accomplish other social purposes and that such standards are usually impossible to achieve.

DIRECTION OF ECONOMIC REGULATORY POLICIES

- Government should continue economic deregulation in areas in which effective competition now exists.

- It is essential that the heavy social costs of public-utility regulation be recognized in cases where it yields only marginal benefits and that regulation be eliminated wherever the real social costs exceed the real social benefits.

- Policy makers should review current antitrust policies, particularly in light of increased world competition, and consider modification of any antitrust laws that inhibit technological development and productivity growth rather than stimulate competitiveness in the international market.

- Government should not permit antitrust policies or other economic regulations to be used to protect individual firms from market forces whenever an individual firm or single industry experiences economic difficulty.

ILLUSTRATION OF HOW MARKET INCENTIVES CAN BE USED

- In implementing regulatory policy, government should encourage the use of the bubble and offsets concepts.
  - The approval process for use of the bubble and offsets programs should be simplified and rapidly accelerated.
  - New as well as old plant and equipment should be eligible for inclusion in the bubble and offsets programs.
  - New-source performance-standard regulations, which now restrict the inclusion of new plant and equipment in the bubble, should be modified by amending the enabling legislation to permit more general use of the innovative bubble concept.

a. These recommendations are based on *Redefining Government's Role in the Market System* and *Productivity Policy: Key to the Nation's Economic Future*.

law to conglomerate mergers have not been successful, and most cases have been dismissed by the courts or dropped by the Antitrust Division. The Antitrust Division has clarified its policies with respect to joint research ventures, stating that it considers many of them to be competitively benign. Since the mid-1970s, antitrust enforcement under both Republican and Democratic Administrations and in the courts has gradually become more economically rational.

For a variety of reasons, many executives have been cautious in interpreting the new direction of antitrust policy and have failed to improve economic efficiency through policies that they believed might be challenged on the basis of antitrust laws. In some cases, this caution has been justified; many court decisions have not been consistent with the current state of thinking among legal and economic scholars. Moreover, the fact that a practice may have the blessing of antitrust enforcement officials does not preclude private plaintiffs from bringing suit or subsequent Administrations from taking a different position. Finally, some executives may not be fully aware of the changes in thinking that have taken place. Others think that any changes that have occurred only scratch the surface of what is required, and that a radical rewriting of the antitrust laws is a necessary part of this country's effort to accommodate itself to the realities of domestic and international competition.

DO ANTITRUST LAWS NEED A MAJOR OVERHAUL?

Many now suggest that a number of the harms once attributed to private efforts to limit competition have been overstated if not mislabeled. In some instances, what was once seen as anticompetitive conduct is now considered benign or even procompetitive. In other cases, competition is much less fragile than formerly believed. For example, the difficulty of negotiating and enforcing price-fixing agreements *even where they are legal* is much better appreciated than it once was. Without some sort of facilitating action by government (such as enforcing sanctions against "cheaters"), cartels are likely to be difficult to form and even more difficult to maintain. Concern about predatory pricing has waned as it has become recognized that pricing strategies once deemed predatory are instead appropriate business conduct and as the notion that a market niche can be secured through predation has come increasingly into question. The once virtually undisputed view that a linkage exists between concentrated markets and excess profits has fallen into serious disrepute. The idea that vertical restrictions on price or other dimensions of competition create additional market power for the firms engaging in them has been largely discredited. The belief that mandatory trebling of antitrust damages is necessary for an appropriate level of antitrust deterrence has been seriously questioned.

Given such changes in economic thinking, plus the growing view that the primary function of antitrust policy is to promote economic efficiency, is there still a case to be made for these laws? Have they outlived their usefulness?

HORIZONTAL AND VERTICAL PRICE-FIXING

The realization that without government sanction and protection, cartels are not easily formed, are not very long-lasting, and may not be very effective does *not* mean that cartels are beneficial for the economy. When successfully formed and enforced, even for a short period of time, they distort markets. **Market forces (as well as antitrust enforcement) may well be useful as a weapon against horizontal price-fixing, but the nation should not relax its antitrust guard against the practice.**

In some countries, cartels have been used to aid in industry restructuring, and some have urged the United States to emulate this practice. However, the record of so-called recession cartels in rationalizing excess capacity in distressed industries and in promoting positive adjustment is almost uniformly disappointing. (See "Crisis Cartels: A Brief Survey of Practices and Experience," page 76.) **Exemptions to the normal blanket prohibition against horizontal price-fixing on the grounds that they will permit the industry in question to restructure itself more efficiently are, in general, not justified.** Congress should seriously consider exemptions *only* if it can be conclusively demonstrated that a proposed restructuring plan (1) would clearly lead to a more competitive domestic industry, (2) could not be carried out without antitrust exemption, and (3) will not lay the groundwork for future collusive action by members of the industry once the restructuring is completed. On the basis of past experience, we believe that most proposals will fail some or all parts of this test.

The treatment of vertical price-fixing poses more complex and difficult questions. The courts now judge most vertical *nonprice* restraints under a rule-of-reason test[2] but consider vertical *price* restraints to be per se illegal. This difference in treatment reflects the courts' growing view that a firm possessing monopoly power does not necessarily extend that power through the use of vertical restraints. Some types of vertical restraints may in fact be *procompetitive*. However, the courts' reluctance to permit vertical price restraints is based on a historical and understandable reluctance to allow price-fixing of any sort.

---

2. A *rule-of-reason test* looks at the impact on competition of particular conduct in a particular case. If the conduct is found to be reasonable in the given context, it is upheld; if not, it is struck down. But no general presumption of the validity or invalidity of the conduct is created.

There are strong arguments for eliminating the per se prohibition against vertical price-fixing. The establishment of *maximum* resale prices might protect consumers against exploitation by dealers with market power.[3] There are also good grounds for believing that in some situations, an inability of manufacturers to restrict price discounting may generate serious free-rider problems;[4] this is more apparent where the product is technologically complex. It is also clear that in practice, it is extremely difficult to differentiate nonprice competition from price competition. Restrictions on one tend to channel competitive energies in the direction of the other.

---

3. This was the clear intent of the conduct struck down in *Albrecht v. Herald Co.*, 390 U.S. 145 (1968).

---

4. The term *free rider* refers to the ability of customers to obtain detailed information on product performance from full-service dealers and then make their purchases from discounters who do not maintain showrooms or staffs of technically trained salesmen. Efforts to limit this problem by charging customers separately for this information have generally proved unsuccessful.

CRISIS CARTELS: A BRIEF SURVEY OF PRACTICES AND EXPERIENCE

The idea of relaxing a nation's antitrust laws in order to assist some or all of its industries through a period of economic crisis is not new. The United States experimented briefly with such a policy during the early years of the Great Depression, and the practice appears to be becoming increasingly prevalent. A recent survey by an OECD Committee of Experts found that Belgium, Denmark, Finland, the Netherlands, Sweden, and Switzerland permit the formation of crisis cartels without prior authorization. Norway, Federal Republic of Germany, Japan, Spain, and the European Economic Community (EEC) also permit crisis cartels, but only after prior authorization.

What are the specific aims of crisis cartels? In the United States during the 1930s, their stated objective was to eliminate "cutthroat competition" and boost prices, thereby helping to restore "business confidence." Their recent use has been stimulated largely by a desire to ease the adjustment burdens of structurally depressed industries needing to shrink capacity but having a difficult time doing so.

How successful have crisis cartels been? In most cases, they have not worked as hoped. This was clearly the case with respect to the U.S. experience. A recent summary of this experience concluded:

Before the end of the first year of the NRA (National Recovery Act, the statute which authorized the antitrust exemptions) codes, the initial enthusiasm for these cartel arrangements clearly shifted to skepticism and criticism. So serious and widespread was the opposition that in January 1934 the NRA's chief administrator held a price hearing to al-

Therefore, if it is considered appropriate to judge *vertical nonprice restraints* on a rule-of-reason basis, it is hard to see why *vertical price* restraints should be treated differently.

On the other hand, legal prohibitions of minimum resale prices have helped to encourage the spread of discounting, which has been desirable for many consumers. Moreover, price restraints may be easier for a firm with monopoly power to enforce and police than nonprice restraints. Therefore, any anticompetitive effects of vertical price agreements may be harder for market forces to deal with than vertical nonprice restraints. Finally, although possibly quite large, the quantitative significance of the free-rider problem is unknown.[5]

---

5. The Small Business Administration has recently solicited research proposals with the aim of providing some estimates of its magnitude. Such research is sorely needed.

---

low critics to present their grievances. Most of the complaints came from government purchasing agents, large retailers, farm organizations, and consumer groups. In a variety of basic industries — lumber, textiles, paper, printing, steel, cement, coal, and scientific equipment — the NRA codes caused uniformity in bids and unjustified price increases. So pervasive were the effects of the codes that one Senator claimed that his office had received over 9000 complaints from small businessmen.

In March 1934, the President created a National Recovery Review Board, headed by the famous criminal trial lawyer Clarence Darrow, to investigate the effect of the codes on small business and recommend any necessary changes. The Board investigated the effects of just eight of the more important codes and found a trend towards monopoly and oppression of small business in practically all of them. Its final report recommended a basic reversal in policy, including the elimination of most price and production provisions. So prevalent was the practice of identical bidding on government contracts that an executive order was issued by the President permitting code members to quote prices to the government up to 15 percent below posted code prices. Further, in some industries, the codes' uniform artificially high prices attracted new entry, expanding production to levels even more wildly in excess of existing demand.[a]

The codes themselves ended with the declaration by the Supreme Court that the National Recovery Act was unconstitutional. Neverthe-

---

a. Organization for Economic Cooperation and Development, *Economic Crisis or Recession and the American Antitrust Laws* (Paris: Organization for Economic Cooperation and Development, Processed, October 1980), pp. 6-7, footnotes omitted.

The current per se standard has the virtue of providing certainty to both manufacturers and distributors, and its retention may make it less expensive (and therefore more feasible) for small retailers to resist manufacturers' efforts to prevent the discounting of their branded merchandise, but the weight of economic evidence is increasingly against its retention. **We support current Justice Department efforts to seek test cases in which the appropriate limits on vertical price arrangements can be probed.** This permits the division to develop a better idea about how an appropriate rule of reason might be formulated. It also permits research of the sort that the Small Business Administration is sponsoring concerning the quantitative significance of the free-rider problem to be conducted. If the courts balk at this approach, or if it ultimately becomes clear that a proper rule of reason cannot be put in place without statutory change, the Administration should consider proposing appropriate legislation.

---

less, their influence lingered. Many of the more prominent examples of price-fixing uncovered by the Justice Department for decades thereafter traced their origins directly to these NRA codes.

In countries where crisis cartels have been employed to aid structurally depressed industries in shrinking their productive capacity, their value has been questionable. The formation of the cartels more often than not has not led to the desired reduction in capacity. The only country that has reported some measure of success in a policy of "controlled shrinkage" of structurally depressed industries is Japan. Eight Japanese industries currently qualify for antitrust exemptions as depressed industries: aluminum, cardboard, cotton and wool spinning, electric-furnace steel, ferrosilicon, fertilizers, shipbuilding, and synthetic fibers. Petrochemicals is likely to be added to this list soon. But even here, the policy's success has been limited, and the role of the antitrust exemption in its attainment has been uncertain.

A few of the industries on the Japanese list — cotton and wool spinning are the best examples — have been the subject of several unsuccessful efforts by the Japanese government to induce controlled shrinkage. Crisis cartel has followed crisis cartel, but capacity has not shrunk as desired. Most of the other industries are newly designated as distressed. They trace their troubles to the oil shocks of 1973-1974 and 1979. Despite clear signals that shrinkage of these industries is necessary, and despite the many inducements available (including, but not limited to, the antitrust exemption), shrinkage has been hard and, indeed, has not always been achieved.

A recent sympathetic account reviewing Japanese efforts in this area stated:

ATTITUDES TOWARD MONOPOLIZATION AND MERGERS

Although monopoly power may be hard to attain, this does not mean that we should be unconcerned about the effects of monopolization. **Recent evidence on the link between concentration and monopoly power does not, in our view, support substantial modification of Section 2 of the Sherman Antitrust Act of 1890. Similarly, the realization that the appropriate relevant market in merger cases (as well as monopolization cases) will often be somewhat broader than the scope of markets once used does not suggest that Section 7 of the Clayton Act of 1914, the nation's principal antimerger statute, should be repealed.**

In interpreting antitrust law (Section 2 of the Sherman Antitrust Act or Section 7 of the Clayton Act), the realities of international competition need to be taken into account. Nothing in current law *precludes* consideration of international competition when defining the relevant market for antitrust

---

Many Japanese managers have refused to go along, which may surprise Westerners who think of Japan as populated entirely by team players. The aluminum industry took so long to cut capacity that it almost cut its throat instead. The leaders of the electric-furnace steel industry, as unbending as their product, have actually increased capacity in the face of the flaccid demand. . . . The salvation of the shipbuilding industry has been the policy's big success story so far. . . . (But even here,) the reduction was hardly smooth sailing. . . . The 61 surviving companies differed sharply about who would cut how much.

The article concludes:

What policy makers — and businessmen — elsewhere can learn from the Japanese experience is that compromise on problems as painful and extensive as collapsing industries doesn't come easy, even in a land known for the willingness of individuals to submerge their interests in the common good.

Nevertheless, the article predicts:

Despite these difficulties — and the obvious danger that misapplied policies could end up merely subsidizing inefficient industries — more and more countries may find themselves imitating the Japanese way.[b]

However, the clear implication of the article is that these other countries should not underestimate the difficulties of achieving even the mixed record of success of Japan.

b. Edward Boyer, "How Japan Manages Declining Industries," *Fortune* 107, no. 1 (January 10, 1983), pp. 58-63.

purposes. However, in the past, antitrust authorities and courts did not always give appropriate consideration to the presence of foreign competitors in formulating domestic antitrust policy and in reaching decisions in particular cases. As in many other areas of antitrust policy, this appears to be changing for the better as evidenced by the Department of Justice's current merger guidelines. **We call upon all relevant government authorities to include in their analysis of market competition all foreign and domestic firms that are active competitors in the domestic market being analyzed.**

The question of how appropriately to take foreign competition into account in defining markets for antitrust purposes is complicated by the differential treatment of domestic and foreign competitive practices under our trade laws. Public policy clearly requires consideration of the influence of actual or potential foreign competitors. For example, a merger of two domestic steel companies can, under appropriate circumstances, represent the legitimate operation of the market as industrial restructuring occurs in response to changing demand. In a monopolization case involving the nation's largest computer maker, or an agreement by a major segment of the domestic semiconductor industry to undertake joint research, the government must consider the effect of foreign competition in deciding whether to raise antitrust concerns.*

U.S. firms can bring complaints against foreign companies under U.S. trade laws, using standards that would not be permissible if applied to domestic competitors, and can thereby limit the effectiveness of this foreign competition.[6] This is a legitimate concern for antitrust authorities. Market definitions for antitrust purposes need to be harmonized with international competitive realities, but it is inconsistent for some to urge statutory and administrative changes aimed at this end and simultaneously to advocate severely restricting the ability of foreign firms to compete in this country on an equal basis with domestic companies. Foreign competitors cannot be counted as full market participants for antitrust purposes if they are excluded from the domestic market through enforcement of our trade laws.

Under a market-based competitiveness strategy, when actual competition from foreign firms exists, mergers and joint research ventures can be a legitimate market response. Unless such restructuring is permitted under our antitrust laws, protectionist pressures will increase.

REDUCING ANTITRUST UNCERTAINTY

The constant threat of private antitrust suits limits the effectiveness of changes in public policy enforcement. Moreover, current opinions are not

---

6. The current definition of *dumping* in all trade laws directs a finding to be made even when the pricing policy being engaged in is identical to what would be considered normal (and socially desirable) pricing practice by domestic firms.

---

*See memorandum by W. BRUCE THOMAS, page 142.

binding on future Administrations. Antitrust advisories, either formal or informal, are nothing more than statements about what those currently charged with enforcing the law believe; they are not legally binding antitrust exemptions.

To reduce this uncertainty, some have proposed giving antitrust advisory opinions the weight of law so that such an opinion, having once been rendered, would bar private suits or suits by subsequent Administrations unless it could be shown that the facts of the case vary from the assumptions of the advisory opinion. Something approaching this was created by the Export Trading Company Act of 1982. Under this statute, companies wishing to engage in export-related practices about which there might be antitrust concerns can describe such practices to the Antitrust Division and, if they are approved, can receive a certificate of review. This certificate does not bar a private antitrust suit. But it does limit any such suit to a civil action for injunctive relief, actual damages, interest on actual damages, and the cost of the suit. Moreover, any private party bringing an *unsuccessful* action against a firm or group of firms having received a certificate of review is to be charged with the costs incurred by the defendant in defending the suit.

Although this represents an important first step toward turning the informal, nonbinding antitrust review into an action having the force of law, it would be incorrect to assume that going the rest of the way would represent only a minor extension of policy. For one thing, exporters have long enjoyed favored status under the antitrust laws. The practical significance of the additional protection provided by the certificate of review may be minor. Moreover, reviews under the procedures set up by the Export Trading Company Act have just begun. Even at this early stage, there are signs that the review process may not work as smoothly or be as attractive to business as its proponents had wished.

One problem with this type of certification procedure is that it is likely to become more complex if generally applied. The advocates of binding clearance procedures usually envision retaining the extreme informality of the current business review process while cloaking the outcome of this process with the force of law, but this may be an unrealistic hope. Although there may be occasions on which such a hybrid procedure would prove acceptable, it is unlikely that it would be generally palatable to the courts and Congress. Transforming the Antitrust Division from its current status as primarily a prosecutorial body into what in effect would be a regulatory agency with the power to issue legally binding decisions would almost certainly be accompanied by a requirement that the agency adopt the trappings characteristic of other regulatory bodies: a formal record, opportunity for comment by affected parties, the necessity of a formal decision with stated findings, and the possibility even of judicial review. Such a process would eliminate much of the value and ease of informal antitrust review. It also might lead to an extremely cautious attitude on the part of antitrust officials in granting clearances.

The process of granting case-by-case, legally binding antitrust exemptions for the proposed activities of export trading companies is just beginning. **Before enacting legislation which would establish general procedures that would turn antitrust advisory opinions into legally binding antitrust exemptions, there should be an opportunity to evaluate experience in the one area where such procedures are currently being implemented.**

PRIVATE ANTITRUST SUITS

Private suits far outnumber suits brought by the Antitrust Division and Federal Trade Commission combined. Furthermore, it is clear that the aim of many private suits is the suppression rather than the promotion of competition. Companies sometimes use the threat of a private antitrust suit to deter rivals from taking actions that are perfectly justified and, indeed, procompetitive. Some state and local officials have used antitrust suits of dubious merit to support their political ambitions. Furthermore, private antitrust suits complicate, and often impede, the development of sound and consistent antitrust doctrine. Cases are not brought with an eye toward their strategic policy importance or their deterrent effect but for the immediate advantage of private parties.

This does not mean that the right to seek private antitrust remedies should be repealed. They clearly have a legitimate role to play in enforcement, especially where the conduct involved is generally accepted as anticompetitive and the results are clearly adverse to the public interest. The federal government has neither the resources nor the incentive to be the sole enforcer of the antitrust laws. Consumers, competitors, or other private parties who can prove legitimate injury should not be barred from the possibility of having their day in court.

The popularity of private antitrust litigation is promoted by the availability of contingent fee arrangements and the general presumption in U.S. law against assessing costs (and possibly even damages) against parties who bring unsuccessful suits. Without major changes in the way society views legal remedies, nothing is likely to be done about contingent fee litigation. However, as already noted, there are signs that attitudes concerning the award of legal costs are changing. The Export Trading Company Act of 1982 introduced into U.S. antitrust law the threat that private plaintiffs will be charged the costs of unsuccessful actions. **We recommend that Congress consider legislation that would broaden the application of this policy. Its**

use seems especially appropriate in those cases where defendants have relied on antitrust advisory opinions as having the force of law or where conduct is carried on openly in the belief that it is legal. Also encouraging in this regard are the recent efforts by the U.S. Supreme Court to impose costs on parties bringing frivolous appeals.[7] Access to the courts should not be denied to any citizen, but those availing themselves of this access should be forced to bear the costs of using it frivolously. An effort should be made to develop a consensus aimed at imposing costs on those who use the courts for this purpose.

A problem unique to some antitrust litigation is the ability of injured private parties to collect automatically three times the damages that they can demonstrate they have sustained. Although it may not be the case that appropriate deterrence will be achieved merely by confining private awards to single damages, given the low probability of detection of many antitrust offenses, the automatic award of treble damages is clearly contrary to the public interest. It deters firms from openly undertaking conduct that they believe is either procompetitive or benign. As we have seen, the Export Trading Company Act of 1982 also breaks ground here by limiting the damages that parties proving a violation of antitrust law can collect. **Policies to limit the award of treble damages to those instances in which conduct is a per se violation and is carried out in secret (such as price-fixing) should be adopted by Congress. At the very least, judges should be given discretion in multiplying damage awards, with prescribed guidelines.**

IMMUNIZATION OF JOINT RESEARCH ACTIVITIES

Joint research ventures are currently judged under a rule of reason. Factors favorable to approval include a focus on research rather than on the development end of the spectrum, low or moderate combined market shares of the participants, and open access if it is essential to competitive survival. The willingness of the Antitrust Division to grant approval to the proposed joint research venture of several of the nation's largest semiconductor companies illustrates the flexibility inherent in the current process.

Recently, the Administration proposed legislation that might give such ventures a modest additional degree of protection. It has proposed codification of existing practice by prohibiting the courts from declaring illegal per se any joint research venture or any agreement concerning the licensing of intellectual property (i.e., a patent or a trademark). It would limit the award

---

7. The case involved a student who considered himself discriminated against and who insisted on filing an appeal with the Supreme Court even though he had lost at all other levels. In dismissing his appeal, the Court assessed the student $500 in costs. The case has been widely viewed as a warning that the Court is prepared to impose much higher cost awards in the future for frivolous appeals.

of damages for conduct by a joint research arrangement that eventually is found illegal by the courts *provided* the activities of the arrangement have been fully disclosed to the Antitrust Division. Damages that can be assessed for anticompetitive conduct with respect to the licensing of intellectual property would also be limited. Finally, the scope of what might be deemed misuse of an intellectual property right would be limited.

A greater degree of joint research than firms in this country have engaged in the past is desirable. There is a widespread perception that present antitrust rules can inhibit worthwhile ventures, if only because their application is uncertain. Although the Administration's policy may include help in this regard, a proposal for formal review and clearance procedure deserves serious consideration by Congress.

INTERNATIONAL CONSIDERATIONS

The United States has a longer tradition of vigorous antitrust enforcement than any other country in the world. Although antitrust restrictions are becoming increasingly significant in some foreign jurisdictions, it is still fair to say that the rules are tougher in this country. In a world where international competition is increasingly the norm, some have questioned whether our antitrust statutes, even if appropriate for the United States, have become a hindrance to our ability to compete internationally.

The differences in antitrust rules are extremely distressing to some American business executives. They see foreign firms with which they compete in this country engaging in actions in their own countries that would be patently illegal here. They also observe foreign governments acting to limit the efforts of U.S. authorities to prosecute foreign firms for actions taken outside the United States that have significant competitive impact here.

Such concern is understandable. However, it should be tempered by the recognition of a number of important facts. First, the ability of firms to engage in apparently anticompetitive conduct in their home countries does not necessarily imply that they gain an important competitive advantage here or abroad. The economic reasoning which holds that even *legal* cartels are often ineffective applies with equal force to the actions of foreign cartels. Second, U.S. trade laws provide some protection against the actions of foreign cartels. If foreign firms conspire to lower prices in a predatory manner, our antidumping laws provide remedies. (Indeed, the standard of proof required to establish predatory pricing by foreign firms is weaker than the one historically applied in domestic monopolization and price discrimination cases.) Third, the United States also employs a differential standard as far as anticompetitive conduct is concerned. The Webb-Pomerene Act, for example, permits U.S. firms to form export cartels and engage in behavior that would be a per se violation if it was directed at commerce within the United States. The only requirement is that actions by Webb-Pomerene associations must not affect U.S. commerce; that is, the actions of such associations must not be a cover for efforts to control competition within the United States. The Export Trading Company Act is another example of differential antitrust application by this country.

ANTITRUST AS AN ELEMENT IN COMPETITIVENESS STRATEGY: SUMMARY

Some have argued that outmoded antitrust policies bear a large share of the blame for this country's decline in international competitiveness. Others charge that any modifications of antitrust enforcement will lead to an era in which monopolies will run rampant throughout the economy. Both views are unjustified. Antitrust retains an important place in the nation's competitiveness strategy in spite of the fact that other countries choose not to have similar policies. The better understanding that has emerged over the past decade about what is and what is not anticompetitive conduct has pointed the way toward a more realistic assessment of what antitrust policy can be expected to achieve. The antitrust laws need not be dismantled, but the changes in antitrust enforcement policy and the statutory reforms that we have suggested here are certainly worthy of consideration.

Chapter 6

Facilitating Adjustment to Changing International Competitiveness

International trade policy is an integral part of U.S. competitiveness. A liberal and open world trading system contributes to better national economic performance by encouraging the movement of labor and other resources toward the most efficient and competitive sectors. Conversely, government interventions, whether in the form of explicit subsidies to particular industries or implicit subsidies through import protection, can adversely affect the performance of the economy by distorting the allocation of resources and the structure of industry.

In certain circumstances, GATT regards government intervention in international trade as legitimate. Intervention for reasons of national security and to counter unfair trade practice are widely accepted. (These actions are discussed in Chapters 4 and 7 respectively.) There are two other reasons for government intervention: First there is the *safeguard case*, in which the government intervenes to prevent serious and perhaps even fatal injury to domestic producers from a large and rapid increase in competing imports of a particular product. Second, government intervention to protect infant industries is accepted as a justifiable course of action by developing nations.

DOMESTIC SAFEGUARDS

Temporary protection to facilitate adjustment to import competition involves a number of problems. Such protection may minimize adjustment costs by allowing for the orderly movement of resources out of the industry by attrition, or it may give management and labor time to improve the efficiency of production to compete with foreign rivals. On the other hand, protective measures may in practice discourage adjustment or encourage resources to move into the sheltered domestic industry because of higher product prices and improved profits. Indeed, because the costs of such protection are not highly visible and are borne by many groups in society, it is easier for specific recipients of protection to succeed in making temporary protection virtually permanent.

However, there have been instances when temporary protection has permitted management to increase productivity and has given labor time to move to alternate employment. But in general, innovation does not thrive if industry is protected from competition. In addition, protection frequently delays labor market adjustments. Terminating protection has become extremely difficult, as the case of textiles and clothing demonstrates. An additional problem with import restrictions is that they typically provide blanket protection to all firms in an industry, including those that may be efficient enough to be viable without them.

However imprecise and hard-to-manage safeguards may be, virtually all countries include them in their arsenal of government weapons to ease domestic adjustment to import competition. In the United States, an "escape clause" is contained in the Trade Adjustment Act authorizing the President to impose import restrictions not otherwise permitted. An extremely important provision of this law is that escape-clause relief is temporary. Import restrictions may be granted for a maximum of five years, must be phased down beginning with the third year, and can be renewed for only one three-year period if considered necessary.

Apart from the substantive standards, the procedures for escape-clause action are quite cumbersome. This complexity is partly intentional; it shields the President to some extent from direct political pressures. Petitions for import relief are filed with the International Trade Commission (ITC). If the commission finds, on the basis of its studies and public hearings, that increased imports are, or threaten to be, a substantial cause of serious injury, it must recommend import restrictions or adjustment assistance. If it recommends import relief, the President has the option of accepting the recommendation, rejecting it, or substituting his own remedy, such as an orderly marketing agreement, an avenue not open to the ITC. If the President does not accept the recommendation, Congress can override the President's decision.

As the recent auto case shows, however, the President can arrange for trade restrictions even when the ITC recommends *against* such action. Because of political pressures and fear that Congress might mandate restrictions legislatively, in 1981 President Reagan negotiated "voluntary" Japanese auto restraints for two years under his general powers to conduct foreign policy. These voluntary restraint agreements, which were extended for a year in both 1983 and 1984, are due to expire in the spring of 1985.

Regardless of the form, safeguards are adopted or negotiated for limited periods. However, strong pressure to extend their duration almost invariably occurs as the expiration date approaches. **This Committee believes that the granting of escape-clause protection should be treated as an exception to the general policy of treating firms as risk-taking enterprises, allowing them to succeed or fail on the basis of traditional market principles.** When government grants such an exception, the industry should be judged on the basis of its demonstrated efforts to regain competitiveness through such actions as modernization, consolidation, phase-down, or phase-out of operations and relocation of production facilities. Progress on implementation of firms' documented actions should be required so long as imports are restricted. Moreover, any extension of protection beyond the initial period should be granted only in the most unusual circumstances and should depend on the degree to which firms in the industry have fulfilled their initial adjustment plans.

AN INTERNATIONAL SAFEGUARDS CODE

In most countries, the legislative and procedural restraints against import restrictions are much weaker than those in the United States. Actions already taken, often in the shape of informal, quantitative limits on imports, have not only distorted the internal use of resources but also have significantly constrained the exports and economic growth of the developing countries. **It is of the utmost importance to the long-run interests of all trading countries that an effective international safeguard code be negotiated and implemented. By making restrictive trade actions subject to reasonable, mutually agreed-upon standards and to multilateral review and discipline, such a code would make it easier for politicians in all countries to resist domestic protectionist pressures.**

The existing international rule of safeguards is contained in GATT Article XIX, the so-called escape clause (adopted in 1947 in the original GATT and unchanged). It permits member countries to impose import restrictions in the case of actual or threatened serious injury to domestic producers despite any GATT obligations to the contrary.

To the extent that countries have formally invoked Article XIX, they have done so increasingly through quantitative import restrictions rather than tariffs. The preference for quotas is due mainly to the greater certainty of their protective effects. At any given time, it is theoretically possible to specify a rate of duty that will reduce imports to exactly the same extent as any given quota; but in practice, the precise effects of the tariff on import volume cannot be anticipated. The increased cost of imported goods result- ing from the tariff may be offset by decreased foreign costs due to improved productivity abroad, foreign government subsidies, the willingness of ex- porters to reduce their profit margins, or depreciation of the exporter's currency. Especially under flexible exchange rates, the greater predictabil- ity of quotas makes them a preferred device for producers seeking to protect their home market. In addition, quotas can be applied in ways that are less transparent than tariffs and that lend themselves more readily to discrimi- nating among supplying countries.

Countries imposing restrictions under Article XIX are generally re- quired to give prior notification to, and consult with, affected parties. They must apply the restrictions to all imports of the product on a nondiscrimina- tory basis, and affected exporters can retaliate by withdrawing equivalent trade concessions. Occasionally, countries using Article XIX can forestall retaliation by offering the affected exporting countries compensation in the form of special tariff concessions on other products.

Unfortunately, Article XIX has been widely breached or bypassed. It has rarely been invoked by GATT members other than Australia, Canada, and the United States. European countries, in particular, have avoided using the GATT escape clause in limiting penetration of their markets by Japan and newly industrialized developing countries and have resorted, instead, to nonpublic administrative measures, restrictive industry-to-in- dustry arrangements, and orderly marketing agreements and have induced exporting countries to adopt voluntary export restraints. The United States has also used these techniques, although to a considerably lesser extent than some of the major European countries, including France and the United Kingdom.

In circumventing the GATT escape clause, countries generally avoid the need for a finding of serious injury. Moreover, the trade restrictions are usually discriminatory, applying only to the exports of the strongest competitors. Finally, the restricting country does not incur retaliation or the obligation to compensate the adversely affected countries. *In short, in recent years, the existing international standards, procedures, and penalties for restrictive trade actions have been largely inoperative.*

The negotiation of a modernized safeguard code was high on the agenda of the Tokyo Round, but despite a strong effort by the United States, this effort was not successful. If the danger of a new epidemic of beggar-my-neighbor tactics in international trade is to be avoided, a strengthened set of international rules and procedures for the use of trade restrictions needs to be adopted and put to use.

The main elements of a new safeguard code should ensure that restrictive measures are transparent, limited in scope and duration to what is necessary to prevent serious injury, temporary and phased down during the period of protection, and accompanied by measures to promote structural adjustment to changes in comparative advantage. Resort to restrictive actions should be subject to an improved international discipline that includes a more precise specification for the determination of serious injury and more explicit procedures for taking action.[1]

Because trade issues often become highly politicized, procedures can be as important as substantive standards. Their main purpose should be to alert those whose interests may be adversely affected by the pending restrictions (e.g., importers, consumers, industrial users of the product) and to permit them to exert countervailing pressures on the authorities in the importing countries. Interested parties should be able to present their views and submit relevant evidence in public hearings. Such procedures are commonly lacking outside the United States.

When the safeguard issue was discussed in the Tokyo Round, a central issue turned out to be discrimination. The EEC, in particular, insisted that a new code permit restrictions against selected countries considered the principal source of disruptive imports rather than against all countries. By their very nature, voluntary export restraints are an example of such selective restrictions.

The developing countries have strongly opposed legitimizing selectivity in a new safeguard code; they fear that it would reduce a major con-

---

1. Over the last two decades the use of direct protection techniques, such as quotas and tariffs, to protect industry from foreign competition has declined substantially. However, there appears to have been a substantial increase in the use of indirect, and less visible protective techniques. These include complex administrative regulations placed on imports, domestic subsidies and voluntary agreements among nations. If all countries agreed to document the extent of these techniques they would be much more transparent and their cost more evident.

straint on escape-clause measures, encouraging stronger countries to impose restrictions on weaker nations without risk of significant retaliation of the sort that might occur if the restriction had to be extended to other industrial countries. *A practical compromise on the selectivity issue would be a formula that would not rule out selective restrictions but would make them subject to more stringent substantive and procedural requirements than those that would apply to nondiscriminatory safeguards. All informal restrictive arrangements, including voluntary export restraints, should be required to conform to the provisions of the new code.*

How effective a new international safeguard code would prove in preserving an open world trading system would depend not only on the nature of its legal constraints but also on national policies affecting the capacity of individual countries to accommodate to changing production structures without undue social, economic, and political strain.

CHANGING GLOBAL DIVISION OF LABOR

A critical aspect of a U.S. competitiveness strategy is how this nation adjusts to the rapidly changing global division of labor. As any purchaser of consumer goods such as radios, clothing, and shoes is aware, the developing countries have become important exporters of manufactured products. As this trend intensifies, will the advanced industrial countries, including the United States, make room for the labor-intensive products of the Third World, or will they resist accommodating their industrial structures to the realities of changing comparative advantage?

There is more at stake than gains for all trading countries from a more efficient global use of resources. In a world of interdependent nations, the very stability of the international system depends on opportunities for the less developed countries to realize their economic potential. Particularly in the 1980s, the ability of developing countries to sustain satisfactory growth levels while adjusting to high debt-service and oil-import bills is crucially dependent on their export capabilities.

SHIFT TOWARD THIRD WORLD EXPORTS OF MANUFACTURED GOODS

Prior to World War II, North-South trade conformed broadly to the classical pattern: the exchange of raw materials from the poor countries for the manufactured products of the rich. After the war, this pattern began to change as more advanced developing countries, seeking to industrialize and to conserve foreign exchange, adopted policies to encourage substitution of domestic production for imports of manufactured products.

Later, a number of developing countries, realizing that they needed not simply to save but also to earn more foreign exchange, began to shift their economic strategy from import substitution to export promotion. Import regulations were liberalized, and export subsidies were introduced in attempts to reduce or remove the bias in favor of producing primarily for the home market.

Combining abundant and inexpensive labor with imported capital and technology, a number of developing countries became formidable competitors on world markets for more labor-intensive goods. After 1973, they expanded their exports of manufactured goods in order to service the massive debt they incurred to finance steeply higher oil-import bills. In short, a historic change was brought about in the structure of developing country trade: Whereas manufactured goods constituted less than 16 percent of Third World nonoil exports in 1960, they had increased to more than 52 percent by 1980.[2]

CONCENTRATION OF EXPORTS OF MANUFACTURED GOODS

Although exports of manufactured goods constitute more than half of total nonoil exports from the Third World, most developing countries are still heavily dependent on primary commodities for more than 70 percent of their exports.[3] This seeming paradox is explained by the heavy concentration of exports of manufactured goods in a handful of more advanced developing countries. In 1975, almost 80 percent of Third World exports of manufactured goods came from only eight countries: Hong Kong, Taiwan, South Korea, Yugoslavia, Singapore, Brazil, India, and Mexico. Most other developing countries rely overwhelmingly on exports of basic commodities. Developing-country exports have also been concentrated in a few product categories and industries, over half in just three sectors: textiles, clothing, and electronics and electrical machinery.

Given the widespread popular perception that the developing countries are displacing a substantial portion of domestic manufacturing in the industrial countries, particularly the United States, it is revealing to examine their actual degree of market penetration. The measure conventionally used is the ratio of imports from the developing countries to apparent consumption (defined as domestic production plus imports minus exports).

2. World Bank, *Commodity Trade and Price Trends,* August 1982, p.3.

3. World Bank, *World Development Report,* 1981, Annex Table 9.

As shown in Figure 5, the market share of developing countries in all manufactured goods consumed was only 3.0 percent in the United States and 3.4 percent in the industrial countries as a whole in 1979. However, the extent of market penetration increased rapidly over the 1970s and, as shown in Figures 6 and 7, has been heavily concentrated in particular labor-intensive sectors. For example, the Third World share of industrial country consumption was more than 14 percent for wearing apparel and 15 percent for footwear in 1979 (Figure 7). For the labor-intensive industries within apparel, however, the market penetration percentages are even higher (e.g., 36.5 percent for knitted apparel).

Among the three main industrial centers (the United States, Japan, and Western Europe), the degree of Third World market penetration in manufactured goods has been highest in the EEC (4.7 percent), although for France the share of imports is substantially less than for the EEC areas as a whole (Figure 5). Next comes Sweden, with 4.1 percent, the United States with 3.0 percent, and finally Japan, with 2.3 percent. If, instead of the level of market penetration, we look at the rate at which it has been increasing, we find that the United States is in first place (11.3 percent), the EEC is second (6.4 percent), and Japan is again third (5.5 percent).

Although a small number of countries account for the bulk of exports of manufactured goods from the developing countries, the capacity to produce and export manufactured products is being widely diffused in the Third World. Among the relative newcomers are Malaysia, Thailand, the Philippines, the Ivory Coast, Tunisia, Morocco, Colombia, Uruguay, and Chile. To some extent, the newcomers are replacing the original newly industrialized countries such as Taiwan and Korea in the more labor-intensive products while the latter move up to more skill-intensive fields such as engineering products. In short, the dynamic of comparative advantage is at work among the developing countries as well as among them and the industrial countries.

THIRD WORLD IMPORTS OF MANUFACTURED GOODS

Developing countries import several times more manufactured goods from industrial countries then they export. In fact, the developing countries have been a more rapidly growing market for the manufactured products of the industrial countries than the industrial countries themselves. In part, this large excess of imports over exports reflects the trade of OPEC countries, which are major importers and negligible exporters of such products. Even if OPEC members are excluded, however, the developing countries' imports of manufactured goods from the industrial countries are more than

94

FIGURE 5

Share of Imports in the Apparent Consumption of Manufactured Goods in Industrial Countries, 1970 to 1979

(Percent)

	1970		1979		Growth of Import Shares, 1970-1979	
	All Imports	Developing Country Imports	All Imports	Developing Country Imports	All Imports	Developing Country Imports
Australia	20.8	2.1	24.3	5.3	2.3	12.0
Canada	26.1	2.2	36.3	2.3	3.0	6.6
EEC[a]	18.9	2.7	29.6	4.7	5.3	6.4
Belgium	61.7	5.6	70.7	4.6	1.2	-0.5
France	12.1	2.1	16.0	2.9	3.3	5.0
Federal Republic of Germany	19.3	2.3	30.3	4.5	5.2	8.4
Italy	15.1	2.1	29.3	4.8	7.3	9.3
Netherlands	41.2	4.9	53.6	9.0	3.0	7.2
United Kingdom	16.3	3.3	27.2	5.5	6.3	4.1
Japan	4.5	1.3	5.7	2.3	1.8	5.5
Sweden	31.0	2.8	38.7	4.1	2.3	3.5
United States	5.4	1.2	9.6	3.0	6.6	11.3
Total	10.6	1.7	16.8	3.4	5.1	8.1

[a] Excluding Greece, which joined the EEC in 1981.

SOURCE: Helen Hughes and Jean Waelbroeck, "Can Developing-Country Exports Keep Growing in the 1980s?" *The World Economy* (June 1981). The data are based on a World Bank program of studies of the impact of developing country exports of manufactures on the markets of the industrial countries.

FIGURE 6

Share of Imports in the Apparent Consumption of Manufactured Goods in Industrial Countries by Major Product Groups, 1970 to 1979

(Percent)

Product Group	1970		1979		Growth of Import Shares, 1970-1979	
	All Imports	Developing Country Imports	All Imports	Developing Country Imports	All Imports	Developing Country Imports
Food, beverages, and tobacco	8.6	1.0	10.8	3.9	2.4	2.1
Clothing, textiles, and leather	11.6	2.7	23.8	9.6	7.8	14.8
Wood products	9.5	1.8	16.0	3.8	5.5	7.8
Paper and printing	6.6	0.1	8.7	0.4	3.1	13.4
Chemicals	10.6	2.0	14.9	3.4	3.1	5.2
Nonmetallic minerals	5.9	0.3	9.3	1.0	5.0	13.2
Metals	15.0	3.2	18.4	3.5	2.2	1.4
Machinery	11.3	0.3	21.9	2.0	8.0	21.8
Miscellaneous	18.8	8.0	36.6	18.2	7.3	7.2
Manufacturing	10.6	1.7	16.8	3.4	5.1	8.1

SOURCE: Hughes and Waelbroeck, "Can Developing-Country Exports Keep Growing in the 1980s?"

FIGURE 7

Product Groups With a Developing Country Share of More Than 10 Percent in Apparent Consumption, 1970 to 1979

Item	Developing Country Market Penetration		
	1979	Growth Rate 1970-1979	Total Apparent Consumption (billion)
Vegetable and animal oils and fats	10.9%	0.1%	$40.3
Grain mill products	20.9	3.2	46.6
Sugar products	12.6	−4.0	20.2
Cotton fabrics	10.7	8.3	12.3
Fibers for textile use	13.8	3.4	5.2
Knotted carpets	29.2	4.4	3.1
Cordage, rope, and twine	13.1	7.0	1.8
Wearing apparel	14.1	17.6	84.0
Women's, girls', and infants' outerwear	10.5	22.8	30.0
Underwear	16.9	14.2	11.9
Leather apparel	38.7	17.7	4.0
Headgear	12.7	19.0	0.9
Knitted apparel	36.5	10.7	7.0
Tanned and finished leather	19.3	8.7	6.8
Furs	67.3	15.8	0.4
Manufactured leather	17.2	−19.7	6.9
Footwear	15.6	20.8	18.1
Other nonferrous metals	12.1	−1.2	60.2
Watches and clocks	13.9	45.4	7.1
Jewelry	59.7	5.3	8.6
Toys, ornaments	13.6	20.2	9.6

SOURCE: Hughes and Waelbroeck, "Can Developing-Country Exports Keep Growing in the 1980s?"

two and a half times the value of their exports, and the excess increased from $25 billion in 1973 to $88 billion in 1980.

The United States has shared in the general trend in the industrial countries toward growing surpluses in trade in manufactured products with the developing countries. In 1980, the excess of U.S. exports over imports of manufactured products was $15 billion, excluding trade with traditional oil exporters, and $28 billion in trade with all developing countries. U.S. exports to the developing countries in 1980 ($56 billion) exceed its combined exports to Japan and all of Western Europe ($48 billion) by a substantial margin.[4]

What we are witnessing is a major change in the international division of labor in which the more labor-intensive activities are shifting to countries of the Third World while the industrial countries concentrate increasingly on the production of goods and services embodying higher proportions of capital, technology, and skills. **In our view, this process of international specialization increases the real incomes of all participating countries and dampens the forces of inflation. Therefore, impediments to it should be minimized.**

ADJUSTING TO RISING IMPORTS FROM DEVELOPING COUNTRIES

However much the restructuring of world production benefits all parties over the long run, it does create more immediate problems of adjustment. These can be especially difficult in times of slow growth and high overall unemployment. Job displacement by low-wage foreign labor has become virtually a slogan justifying demands for protection.

EMPLOYMENT EFFECTS AND ADJUSTMENT POLICIES

Many studies have attempted to estimate the number of jobs lost because of imports of manufactured products, but the task is not easy. Jobs lost will depend on the labor intensity of the products being displaced and on the indirect effect on employment in industries supplying the directly affected industry. However, if the market for the product is increasing, it is possible for the ratio of imports to domestic production to rise without necessarily entailing any absolute contraction in domestic employment. In such a case, job loss due to imports is potential, not actual, and there is no problem of adjustment.

---

4. GATT, *International Trade, 1980-81* (Geneva: GATT, 1981), Tables A17 and A22.

In any case, job displacement should be measured against job creation by expanded exports of manufactured products to the developing countries. A recent OECD study concluded that the net effect of expanded exports to developing countries in the 1973-1977 period was to increase employment in the OECD countries by approximately 200,000 jobs annually. [5]

Nevertheless, increased imports can result in the loss of jobs in specific industries and firms, even though the overall effect of increased trade generates employment growth. The ease with which workers affected by this form of structural change move to different jobs depends on actions management and labor, as well as the government, take to encourage those adversely affected. As we pointed out in Chapter 4, however, loss of employment also occurs because of other forms of economic change unrelated to trade. Therefore, public labor market policies should facilitate the reemployment of those affected by economic change regardless of the cause of displacement.

EXCHANGE RATES AND FOREIGN INVESTMENT

International competitive pressures may also arise from, or be accentuated by, exchange rate distortions and from investment incentives and performance requirements by foreign governments.

The sort of extreme competitive pressure which the United States has recently experienced as a result of the undervaluation of the yen has generally not been a problem in relation to developing countries. Developing countries have generally experienced higher rates of inflation than the United States and other industrial countries, and given their persistent current-account deficits, their problem has been mainly one of overvaluation.

Overvaluation is particularly troublesome for the great majority of the developing countries whose currencies are in one way or another pegged to another currency. The most common form of pegging is to the dollar, but a number of developing countries peg to the French franc or other currencies as well as to the special drawing rights. To the extent that the International Monetary Fund (IMF) has attempted to influence the exchange rate policies of developing countries that export manufactured goods, it has generally been to encourage devaluation in order to maintain competitiveness in the face of high inflation rates.

A matter of some concern is the growing worldwide use of foreign investment incentives and performance requirements. *Investment incentives* are designed to attract foreign capital through such government measures

---

5. Report by the Secretary-General, *The Impact of the Newly Industrializing Countries on Production and Trade in Manufactures* (Paris: Organization for Economic Cooperation and Development, 1979).

as tax concessions, cash grants, and customs waivers. *Performance require-ments* are conditions, such as export minimums or local-content require-ments, imposed on the investor by the host government. Such practices can distort the free flow of capital and goods and adversely affect the trade and employment of the investor's home country.

According to a study by the U.S. Department of Commerce,[6] an almost equal percentage of U.S. affiliates in developing and developed countries (27 percent and 25 percent, respectively) have received investment incen-tives. However, a much larger percentage of U.S. affiliates in developing countries have been subject to performance requirements than in devel-oped countries (29 percent versus 6 percent).

The U.S. government has taken various initiatives to restrain incentives and performance requirements. Bilaterally, it has consulted with other gov-ernments in an effort to curb such practices and minimize their detrimental effects. Multilaterally, it has taken the lead in seeking to promote interna-tional discipline in their use. As first steps, GATT is considering an inventory of such practices, and the World Bank has undertaken a study. **We endorse these initiatives and believe they should be followed with a longer-term effort in GATT to develop internationally agreed-upon rules to curb and discipline the use of investment incentives and performance requirements.**

FAIR LABOR STANDARDS

In some industrial countries — notably the United States, the Scandi-navian countries, the EEC — there is considerable sentiment for applying or threatening to apply restrictions against developing countries allegedly guilty of unfair labor practices. Such restrictions are often defended as a means of pressuring employers and governments to adopt more humane and equitable labor laws and practices.[7]

While laudable in principle, the international pursuit of fair labor stan-dards could all too easily strike at the very heart of the reason for trade: com-parative cost differences. To insist that labor in all countries receive any-thing like the same compensation for the same effort and enjoy comparable conditions of work would effectively stop most, if not all, exports from countries producing at lower levels of technology and with less human and physical capital per worker than other countries. This would constitute a clear disaster for most Third World nations.

6. Charlotte A. Zakour, *The Use of Investment Incentives and Performance Requirements by Foreign Governments* (Washington, D.C.: U.S. Department of Commerce, Investment Policy Division, 1981).

7. This section draws on Isaiah Frank, *Trade Policy Issues of Interest to the Third World*, Thames Essay no. 29 (London: Trade Policy Research Centre, 1981).

The drive in some developed countries to use trade policy measures to impose or enforce fair labor standards on low-income countries gains momentum in periods of slow growth. It would therefore be prudent to anticipate such efforts in the decade ahead and to turn them to constructive purposes.

Multilateral development banks are placing new emphasis on basic human needs, social equity, and improved income distribution; these institutions may be able to make an important contribution to improving the conditions of work in developing countries while helping to deflect protectionist pressures based on fair labor standard arguments. **In conjunction with their advisory functions and lending operations, the World Bank and regional development banks should exert influence toward improving labor standards in developing countries in such areas as child labor, safety, health, and the treatment of women.** Of course, standards would have to be sufficiently flexible to accommodate to the conditions in countries of widely divergent social structure and degree of development.

GRADUATION

Developing countries range from countries like Bangladesh and Chad, with per capita incomes below $150 a year, to Brazil and Singapore, with per capita incomes above $2,000.[8] Yet, all these countries, regardless of state of development, are essentially free of the restraints of the generally accepted rules of the international trading system and, in addition, receive favorable treatment in the markets of the industrial countries.

If the industrial countries are to accept the sometimes painful structural adjustments necessitated by the growth of imports of manufactured products from the Third World, it is not unreasonable to expect that the more economically advanced developing countries should begin the process of graduating into fully responsible membership in the international trading community. By *graduation*, we mean the phasing out and ultimate elimination of the differential treatment in trade that the more advanced developing countries now receive and the progressive alignment of their own trade policies with the generally applicable GATT rules.

---

8. World Bank, *World Bank Atlas 1981* (Washington, D.C.: World Bank, 1981). Figures are for 1980. Conversion from national-currency units to dollars is at market exchange rates.

The best-known types of differential treatment now enjoyed by developing countries are the broad right to infant-industry protection and preferential access to the markets of developed countries. In addition, Third World countries are not bound by the prohibition of subsidies on exports of nonprimary products, are relieved of the obligation to offer reciprocal concessions for negotiated tariff reductions, and are virtually exempt from the obligation to refrain from imposing quantitative restrictions for protective purposes. Most developing countries, including some of the most economically advanced, are also free to impose exchange controls on current transactions and to engage in discriminatory currency arrangements without the permission of the IMF.[9]

In order to advance the process of graduation, a new Committee on Graduation should be established in GATT. Its purpose would be to develop both qualitative and quantitative criteria on the basis of which more developed Third World countries would be called upon to forego progressively their special trade privileges and increasingly accept the obligation to abide by the rules that apply to mature international trading partners. Relevant considerations might include such criteria as per capita income, the ratio of manufacturing to total production, and the trend in exports of manufactured products. A graduating country would, of course, retain the right to invoke emergency restrictions for balance-of-payments purposes and any other safeguard provisions generally available to GATT signatories.

More important than the specifics of the arrangements at this stage, however, would be Third World acceptance of the legitimacy of graduation and the serious need for progress in this matter that a new GATT committee would imply.

---

9. Isaiah Frank, "The Graduation Issue for LDCs," *Journal of World Trade Law* 13, no. 4 (July-August 1979): pp. 289-302.

Chapter 7

Unfair International Competition

When U.S. producers petition the government for relief from import competition, a distinction can be made between those cases in which the petitioner does not allege unfair trade practices by the foreign seller (e.g., autos) and those in which such an allegation is made (e.g., steel). The unfair practices generally take the form of dumping or government subsidization, for which established remedies exist in both U.S. and international law.[1]

WHAT IS AN UNFAIR TRADE PRACTICE?

Outside the United States, the term *unfair trade practice* is rarely used because a more interventionist government role in industrial affairs is widely accepted as a matter of course. The term does not appear in GATT or in any of the new international codes negotiated under its auspices. However, Title III of the U.S. Trade Act of 1974 is entitled "Relief from Unfair Trade Practices." It includes specific provisions relating to antidumping duties, countervailing duties to neutralize export subsidization, and measures to counter foreign infringement on U.S. patents. In addition, Title III authorizes the President to retaliate against "unjustifiable," "unreasonable," or "discriminatory" acts of foreign governments that burden or restrict U.S. commerce (Section 301). Retaliation under Section 301 has rarely been carried out, but the provision has been used from time to time and may well be

---

1. The unfair practices addressed in this chapter concern trade in goods. Trade in services is the subject of Chapter 8.

invoked more often in the future to induce foreign governments to rescind certain trade measures deemed in violation of U.S. rights under trade agreements. If some version of the many reciprocity bills that have been introduced in Congress is enacted, pressure to apply Section 301 more frequently would probably increase.

A broader definition of unfair trade practices might include any trade-distorting measures that are inconsistent with internationally accepted norms of behavior. Such a definition would encompass not only dumping and subsidization but also various types of import barriers, including tariffs, quantitative restrictions, and government procurement practices applied in violation of GATT commitments.

EXPORT SUBSIDIES AND DUMPING

MORE UNFAIR THAN IMPORT RESTRICTIONS?

An interesting dichotomy appears in the GATT treatment of trade-distorting devices. Import restrictions, which grant domestic producers an artificial advantage in selling to the home market, are treated more permissively than export subsidies, which grant producers an artificial advantage in foreign markets. The GATT obligation is to try to reduce import tariffs through negotiation, but export subsidies on manufactured products are prohibited outright. Both distort trade and production symmetrically, however: tariffs by drawing excessive domestic resources into the production of goods consumed at home, export subsidies by attracting excessive domestic resources into the production of goods sold abroad. Underlying the differential treatment of import and export distortions is the implicit premise that a country has a greater right to preserve or enlarge its domestic market than to take special measures to penetrate foreign markets.

This line of thinking has undoubtedly led to the use of the expression *unfair trade practices* mainly to categorize export subsidization and dumping. Both have a predatory connotation, whereas measures that are purely protective of the home market have a more benign image. Export subsidization and dumping are similar in that both generally entail selling abroad at lower prices than at home.[2] The main difference is that the former involves some government measures, whereas the latter need not.

---

2. However, neither export subsidies nor dumping need always lead to price discrimination between domestic and foreign markets. In the case of the U.S. Domestic International Sales Corporation (DISC) Act, the export incentive is in the form of partial tax deferral on profits from export sales, a device that may induce a greater export effort without necessarily involving lower-priced sales abroad. Moreover, U.S. law permits a finding of dumping even in the absence of price discrimination between domestic and foreign markets in cases where sales are below the cost of production in the exporting country.

104

WHY NOT SIT BACK AND ENJOY SUBSIDIZED OR DUMPED IMPORTS?

In theory at least, export subsidization and dumping may not be all bad from the standpoint of their effects on the importing country as a whole. It is argued that however unfair these practices may be to producers in the importing country, consumers benefit through the availability of lower-cost products. The traditional answer to this is that the benefits may turn out to be only temporary; once the exporter engaging in such practices has driven out competition and consolidated a large share of the foreign market, he may raise prices above those that would have prevailed under fair competition, and the consumer would suffer in the long run.

The way in which GATT treats export subsidies and dumping reflects a compromise between these views. Export subsidies on manufactured products are proscribed, and the practice of dumping is condemned. But GATT signatories do not automatically have the right to take offsetting action in the form of countervailing or antidumping duties. On the contrary, this right is carefully circumscribed by making the counteraction subject to the additional finding of material injury to an established domestic industry. Because the automatic imposition of offsetting duties is ruled out, consumers are able to enjoy the lower prices in the absence of a demonstration of injury to producers.

Under a grandfather clause exempting existing legislation, the United States was not obliged prior to 1980 to apply the material-injury test as a condition for levying countervailing duties; the test applied only for antidumping duties. As a result of the adoption of a new subsidies code in the Tokyo Round of multilateral trade negotiations, U.S. legislation has been changed to bring it into conformity with the GATT injury test in the case of countervailing duties. However, the test is applicable only to countries that are signatories of the code.

COUNTERING EXPORT SUBSIDIES AND DUMPING

A government can subsidize exports in many different ways. Underlying all the various practices, however, is some artificial benefit to domestic producers for selling in the foreign rather than the home market. All such practices are prohibited except in the case of agricultural products, to which special provisions apply.

Dumping exists when a product is sold for export below its *fair value* and is generally defined as selling at a price below that prevailing in the home market. If no adequate basis exists for determining the home-market price (e.g., when too few domestic sales have been made), the price at which the product is sold to third markets may be used. If neither price standard is available, the *constructed value* of the merchandise is used (i.e., the sum of the cost of producing the product and reasonable additions for overhead and profit).[3]

U.S. law is consistent with the international codes on subsidies and dumping adopted in GATT. In each case, two findings are required before countervailing or antidumping duties may be imposed: a finding by the Department of Commerce of sales at less than fair value and a finding by the International Trade Commission (ITC) of material injury to domestic producers of like products. By and large, the codes and recent U.S. legislation are designed to improve the administration of countervailing and antidumping measures by provisions that are intended both to prevent abuse of these restrictive actions and to expedite enforcement by shortening the time limits for the various stages in the complex process of administering the statutes. In recent years, a considerable number of subsidy and dumping cases have been filed in the United States, although only a modest number have satisfied all the statutory conditions and resulted in the assessment of duties.[4]

In order to make the administration of our unfair trade laws more effective, the reporting system and information base for subsidies and dumping should be improved.

THE STEEL CASE

Steel has been the most important U.S. industry that has been active in seeking relief from foreign dumping and subsidization. In order to discourage the dumping of steel into the U.S. market, the government adopted the trigger price mechanism early in 1978. The idea was to expedite administration of the antidumping law by establishing a reference, or trigger, price as a basis for monitoring imports to determine whether prima facie evidence of dumping exists. The reference price was based on estimated costs of production in Japan, the lowest-cost producer. Any imports below that price would automatically trigger an antidumping investigation by the U.S. government. In return for this mechanism, the steel industry agreed to suspend its dumping charges against European producers, an action that would have poisoned U.S.-European trade relations and might have jeopardized the conclusion of the multilateral trade negotiations.

---

3. Under current U.S. law and regulations, constructed value is also used if a significant percentage of home-market sales is found to be below the calculated cost of production. This rule can lead to questionable results during recessions, when it is not uncommon for firms to be losing money.

---

4. A full listing of antidumping and countervailing duty actions in 1981 is given in the *Twenty-Sixth Annual Report of the President of the United States on the Trade Agreements Program 1981-1982* (Washington, D.C.: U.S. Government Printing Office, 1982), pp. 188, 190.

Early in 1982, the trigger price mechanism was dropped as the steel industry reinstituted complaints of unfair trade practices against European producers under both the antidumping and the countervailing duty statutes.[5] Findings of dumping and export subsidization were made by the Commerce Department, and material injury to domestic producers was found by the ITC. In an effort to forestall mandatory imposition of stiff import penalties, the Department of Commerce succeeded in negotiating quota limitations for European steel shipments in October 1982.

This orderly marketing agreement promised to yield more certain and comprehensive limits on steel imports than would have resulted from pursuing the normal remedies. There is now a strong likelihood that the restrictive arrangements will be extended to other foreign suppliers, including Japan and the developing countries. The result could be a world steel agreement along the lines of the protective and long-lasting Multifibre Agreement that has constrained the growth of international trade in textiles and clothing.

As a matter of general policy, orderly marketing agreements to limit imports are clearly a second-best solution to the problem. Because the protection provided may simply delay the inevitable adjustment to economic change, orderly marketing agreements should be avoided whenever possible. In most cases, the appropriate remedies for unfair trade practices exist in U.S. antidumping and countervailing duty statutes and in comparable provisions of international law contained in GATT. Unlike quota restrictions, the additional duties that may be levied under a reasonable application of these rules would preserve the market mechanism and avoid the rigidity of quantitative limitations on international trade. **However, U.S. laws on unfair trade practices should be enforced more vigorously and expeditiously than in the past. They should also be brought into line with any negotiated changes in the international rules that would permit current countervailing action to offset the advantages of earlier subsidization causing material injury to domestic firms.**

EXPORT CREDITS

In the present highly competitive international economic environment, the importance of official export financing has greatly increased. Countries vie with each other in granting their firms concessional financing in order to gain new foreign markets or to maintain historical market shares for key industries.

---

5. Actually, the mechanism had been suspended for a period in 1980 when the U.S. steel industry filed dumping charges against European producers. It was reinstituted in October of that year, when the petitions were withdrawn.

Although official credits at below-market rates are clearly export subsidies, the subsidies code negotiated in the Tokyo Round provided an exception for countries party to an international agreement on export credits and adhering to the agreement's interest rate provisions. At present, all the major market economies are signatories of the OECD Agreement on Export Credits.

The latest version of this agreement took effect on October 15, 1983. It provides a schedule of minimum interest rates and maximum repayment terms that may be extended to different categories of borrowing countries defined in terms of their per capita GNP. Relatively rich countries (per capita GNP over $4,000) may not be extended credits below 12.15 to 12.40 percent, depending on the loan maturity. The minimum interest rate for poor countries (per capita GNP below $1,000) was set at 9.5 percent for all maturities. Intermediate countries are subject to minimum rates between the two extremes. Because interest rates in Japan have been below these percentages, a special rate has been established for official credits in yen. Minimum rates are subject to an automatic adjustment mechanism.

Although the OECD agreement is a step forward, there is still leeway for foreign subsidization of export financing. For example, the rules have been circumvented through the use of *mixed credits*, a type of concessional financing that blends official export credits with grant aid.[6] Under these circumstances, **the United States strategy should be twofold. In the short run, the U.S. Export-Import Bank should be endowed with sufficient resources to match below-market terms offered by foreign export credit agencies to their exporters.** Consistent with this recommendation, CED endorses the recent authority given to the Export-Import Bank to supply mixed credits to U.S. exporters. **We urge that the United States use this new authority by blending Export-Import credits with credits from the Agency for International Development.** Such efforts to match the practices of other countries should be used as leverage to achieve international agreement on a long-run solution to the problem of export credits. **Over the longer run, however, further multilateral reduction and eventual elimination of export credit subsidies should be sought.** It is fundamentally irrational to grant foreign buyers more favorable credit terms than those available to domestic purchasers. It would be preferable, by far, for the major trading countries to agree to an effective ban on export subsidization so that no country would gain an unfair advantage.

---

6. The Development Assistance Committee of OECD announced on June 14, 1983 (Press Release A/(83)/30) the adoption of guiding principles to discourage trade distortion through the use of mixed credits. It remains to be seen how effective the principles will prove in practice.

DOMESTIC SUBSIDIES

Unlike export subsidies and dumping, which are subject to very specific internationally agreed-upon constraints, GATT permits the payment of subsidies not related specifically to exports.[7] The recently negotiated subsidies code goes even further, explicitly acknowledging the legitimacy of domestic subsidies as instruments of industrial policy.[8]

PURPOSES AND FORMS OF DOMESTIC SUBSIDIES

The code illustrates the types of objectives for which domestic subsidies may legitimately be used: mitigating economic and social disadvantages of specific regions, facilitating the restructuring of certain industrial sectors, encouraging retraining and shifts in employment, redeploying industry for environmental reasons, and promoting research and development, especially in high-technology fields.

The code recognizes the wide diversity of forms of domestic subsidization to achieve these objectives, including tax incentives, government provision of utility services or other support facilities, government subscription to equity capital, government financing of research and development, and grants, loans, or guarantees to commercial enterprises. These techniques of subsidization have been widely used (e.g., in Japan and France) in targeting specific industries for special support and development.

WHY ARE DOMESTIC AND EXPORT SUBSIDIES TREATED DIFFERENTLY?

Why does the GATT code take such a tolerant view of domestic subsidies but prohibit outright export subsidies outside the agricultural sector? After all, if a country subsidizes its exports, it places foreign producers at a disadvantage only in their home market and in third-country markets; but if it subsidizes domestic production, foreign producers may face increased competition not only in their home market and in third-country markets but also in the market of the subsidizing country.

The answer to this question has to do mainly with the purposes of the two categories of subsidies. Export subsidies are devices for gaining a trade advantage over foreign competitors. They provide no particular incentive when domestic producers sell in the home market. In contrast, domestic subsidies provide evenhanded incentives for producing for the home or foreign market. There is at least a presumption, therefore, that the main pur-

---

7. GATT, Article III-8-b and Article XVI.

---

8. Subsidy/Countervailing Duty Code, Article 11-1.

pose of domestic subsidies is not to gain a trade advantage, but to achieve the broader social and economic objectives of industrial policy.

Government intervention through general, sectoral, or regional aid is pervasive in modern economies. Generally, the interventions are justified by the need to correct market imperfections. For example, general subsidies for research and development can compensate for the failure of the market to permit private firms to capture the full benefit of discoveries that may lie at least partly in the public domain. Regional subsidies may induce firms to locate in depressed areas, which may be more costly from the firm's point of view but which advances certain broad social objectives. Subsidies to a particular sector, say nonconventional energy production, may be designed to compensate domestic producers for helping to advance the national objective of energy independence, a contribution not adequately reflected in the market price of fuel. In the United States, substantial subsidization of high-technology sectors has occurred in conjunction with space and defense activities.

INTERNATIONAL TREATMENT OF DOMESTIC SUBSIDIES

It would be politically out of the question to seek to prohibit domestic subsidies through an international code on the grounds that the measures have incidental trade-distorting effects, and it would be impractical to encourage the widespread unilateral application of countervailing duties against measures internationally accepted as legitimate exercises of national sovereignty unless material injury can be demonstrated. An alternative for reconciling national industrial policies (as expressed through domestic subsidies) with a liberal international trading system would be to harmonize such policies so that similar incentives would apply to all countries. However, so long as individual countries have different preferences about the role of government in their economies, it would seem desirable in a pluralistic world that such differences should be accommodated in a manner that minimizes intrusion.[9]

It is in this spirit that the new GATT code on subsidies and countervailing duties deals with domestic subsidies. While acknowledging their legitimacy as industrial policy tools, it recognizes their possible adverse effects on a country's trading partners. A particular domestic subsidy of a code signatory is therefore open to challenge by another signatory on the grounds that the subsidy causes injury to its domestic industry, nullifies or impairs benefits to which it is entitled under GATT, or otherwise seriously prejudices its interests. The code provides mechanisms of consultation, concilia-

9. Richard N. Cooper, "U.S. Policies and Practices on Subsidies in International Trade" in *International Trade and Industrial Policies*, ed., Steven J. Warneke (New York: Holmes and Meier, 1978), p. 118.

tion, and dispute settlement, including provision for recommendations by a committee of signatories. If the committee's recommendations are not followed, it can authorize appropriate countermeasures.

Taken as a whole, the new code represents an enlightened attempt to reconcile national industrial policies with the requirements of a liberal international trading system. It implicitly recognizes that the outright prohibition of all domestic subsidies is neither desirable nor feasible but that an adjudication mechanism is needed when another country believes itself adversely affected. So long as the subsidy's costs are borne mainly by the subsidizing country and only to a minor extent by its trading partners, the matter would presumably not even come up in GATT. Where major adverse effects are claimed, the code provides a practical basis for ad hoc consideration and adjudication.

International discipline over subsidies could be strengthened in three ways. First, potentially troublesome domestic subsidies should be defined. The result would be comparable to the "Illustrative List of Export Subsidies" in the present code. Such a list should specify conditions under which subsidies are not legally troublesome because they offset, in the least objectionable manner, market distortions in specific sectors. Governments should be required to report to GATT all domestic subsidies conforming to the list.

Second, effective remedies for subsidization affecting competition in third-country markets should be developed. Clearly, this problem cannot be met through the device of countervailing duties, which can only offset unfair competition in the importing country's home market. One suggestion is to permit the injured party to grant countervailing subsidies, possibly financed by a special tax on its imports from the subsidizing country.[10]

Third, new rules should be developed to provide more effective remedies for the adverse effects on other countries of government targeting of particular domestic industries for special assistance and support. This is often referred to as "the Japan problem," but it is the broader issue of infant-industry support, recognized as legitimate for developing countries, being granted by developed countries. Generally, the assistance is given to high-technology industries, such as computers and aircraft, to get them launched, help them overcome initial obstacles, and offset early development costs.

The reason current remedies are inadequate is that the damage to com-

---

10. Gary C. Hufbauer, "Subsidy Issues After the Tokyo Round," *Trade Policy in the Eighties*, William Klein, ed. (Washington, D.C.: Institute for International Economics, 1983), p. 355.

peting industries in other countries may not occur for many years, by which time the subsidization will have become redundant and will have been withdrawn. Moreover, there may be no quantitative link, as assumed in the countervailing duty concept, between the amount of the original subsidy and the extent of the current injury. Appropriate revisions of the GATT subsidies code and U.S. policy are therefore needed to cope with this problem.

In devising new rules, great caution should be exercised to minimize the possibilities of abuse. For example, most of the competitive pressures from Japan arise not from targeting and subsidization but from other factors, including more favorable wage rates, more rapid productivity growth, better quality control, and at present, the strong dollar. **Any new rules enlarging the scope for countervailing action should require demonstration of a strong causal link between the targeted subsidies in the exporting country and the material injury in the importing country.**

Because of the nature of the problem of domestic subsidies, it is not possible to lay down outright prohibitions, as in the case of export subsidies. The *effects* of the subsidies must be determined, and a large element of judgment is inevitable in the process. Therefore, **in addition to the proposed substantive changes in the code, we recommend a strengthening and streamlining of the GATT consultation, conciliation, and dispute-settlement procedures.** The measures agreed to at the November 1982 GATT ministerial meeting are welcome steps in this direction.

Ultimately, a revised subsidy code and improved dispute-settlement procedures could evolve into a pragmatic system of precedent and case law on domestic subsidies that could make a major contribution to reconciling national industrial policies with the requirements of an open world trading system.

The use of domestic targeting techniques for developing high-technology industries with export potential is leading to pressure to protect industries in which the United States currently has a comparative advantage. **We recommend that the government establish offices to monitor innovation and competition policies in each major country. These offices could report to the U.S. Trade Representative and the Secretary of Commerce on foreign subsidy practices and determine whether they pose a threat to U.S. industries that requires government action.**

Such an information system would constitute an early warning that the U.S. government is seriously concerned about foreign subsidies and will consider unfair trade remedies. It is also likely to encourage our trading partners to participate in developing a more effective domestic subsidy code in the interest of all trading nations.

112

STATE ENTERPRISES

Among the most difficult problems confronting the new codes are
those related to state enterprises. In the industrial countries, total or partial
public ownership in many industries is common, for example, shipbuilding
(West Germany, Italy, Spain, Sweden, United Kingdom), automobiles
(France, Italy, West Germany, United Kingdom), and steel (United Kingdom, France, Belgium, Italy, Spain, Sweden). State-owned enterprises are
rapidly increasing their market shares in minerals, petrochemicals, aluminum, fertilizers, transportation, and communications. A recent study estimates that state trading accounts for 10 to 15 percent of the foreign trade of
advanced countries.[11]

Advantages of state-owned enterprises include the fact that their initial
capital may be provided partially or totally by the government. Because
their losses are commonly absorbed by the government and profitable firms
may not be required to earn "market" returns, they are able to take greater
risks than private companies can, especially in developing expensive new
equipment such as commercial aircraft and power reactors. Borrowing may
be made easy through direct government loans or loan guarantees. Special tax exemptions and preferential government procurement are also
common.

With these forms of subsidy, state-owned enterprises can become formidable competitors on world markets. Many U.S. firms that compete with
state-owned enterprises in large-scale projects often find themselves at a
competitive disadvantage because the initial risk in such projects is borne
by the foreign government. With capital subsidies, state-owned enterprises
tend toward capital-intensive techniques with high fixed costs. In periods of
weak domestic demand, moreover, they may be obliged to retain their labor force. Since labor also becomes a fixed cost, the incentive to cut prices
in world markets is often intense.[12]

The international competitive distortions arising from the operations of
state enterprises are not limited to subsidization and dumping. State enterprises are also potent instruments for protecting older domestic industries
under pressure from foreign competition and for promoting new industries

11. M.M. Kostecki, "State Trading," in *State-Owned Enterprises in Western Economies*, ed. R. Vernon
and Y. Aharoni (New York: St. Martin's Press, 1981), p. 173.

12. R. Vernon, "Introduction," in *State-Owned Enterprises in Western Economies*, ed. Vernon and
Aharoni, p. 29.

embodying the latest sophisticated technology.[13]

In principle, the international economic problems raised by state enterprise fall within the scope of the new subsidies code, particularly those provisions dealing with domestic subsidies.[14] It is open to serious question, however, whether the new code can prove adequate to the task of dealing with the rapidly expanding phenomenon of state enterprises. **If the code proves inadequate, special rules to inhibit unfair trade practices by state-owned enterprises should be developed and adopted in GATT.**

PERFORMANCE REQUIREMENTS

Another problem of increasing concern is the spread of trade distortions resulting from performance requirements placed on foreign-controlled enterprises by host governments. Such requirements are imposed to ensure that incoming direct investments advance particular national goals such as increasing employment, stimulating industrialization, or improving the balance of payments. These objectives are commonly pursued through trade-related performance requirements in the form of minimum export levels or local-content requirements.

If such requirements pressure firms toward economic behavior inconsistent with market forces, they may distort trade and investment flows, lead to uneconomic use of resourses, and harm the economic interests of other countries. The effects of minimum export requirements are similar to those of export subsidies; they artificially increase exports above levels that would have prevailed in the absence of the intervention. Such exports may displace another country's home production or its sales to third markets.

---

13. No clearer statement of these purposes is needed than that made by French President Francois Mitterrand in his first press conference after taking office:

> I am opposed to an international division of labor and production, a division decided far from our shores and obeying interests that are not our own. We are not a pawn in the hands of those who are more powerful than we. This must be made clear, and for us, nationalization is a weapon to protect France's production apparatus. . . .

> We have to win back the market at home. I return to this point, I want to emphasize it; it is going to be a key policy objective for the seven years of my term. Let me run over some of the guidelines: We have to conquer or reconquer the steel, aluminum and plastics sectors; we have to build a machine-tool industry, integrated circuits, data processing focusing particularly on micro-computers and micro-processors. I intend to see Paris become a world center that will attract the most sophisticated technologies and, as the expression goes, the finest brains.

Francois Mitterrand, Press Conference at Elysee Palace, Paris, September 24, 1981.

---

14. A separate GATT provision on state-trading enterprises is included in the original Article XVII. It is limited to ensuring that a state enterprise treats foreign buyers and sellers in nondiscriminatory fashion.

Losses by the foreign enterprise in such uneconomic exports can usually be made up by exploiting protected positions in the host country.

Local-content requirements artificially reduce imports by mandating that a given percentage of the value of the final product be produced locally or purchased from local sources. These value-added requirements are equivalent to import quotas. Often the two types of requirements are combined by linking a firm's permitted imports to the value of its exports so that no net foreign exchange costs are entailed by its operations.

Performance requirements are enforced through a variety of incentives and disincentives. Foreign enterprises that do not comply may be barred from a host country or may be subject to various penalties. Conversely, incentives such as tax concessions or special grants may be offered to firms willing to adhere to performance requirements. The requirements may be formal in the sense that they are contained in published statutes or regulations or informal and unpublished but carried out through confidential administrative action.

THE EXAMPLE OF THE AUTOMOTIVE INDUSTRY

In the manufacturing sector, trade-related performance requirements are most common in the automotive industry. Typically, a multinational auto company decides to make the best of a host country's requirement that its operations entail zero net foreign exchange costs by adapting its worldwide sourcing of components. Thus, the company may decide to produce a particular component, such as an engine, in the host country for its worldwide operations. After allocating the engines needed for locally built vehicles, the company exports the remainder to its other units. These exports generate foreign exchange credits for the subsidiary in the host country, permitting it to import components from other countries. In short, what is developing in the world automotive industry is a pattern of international investment and trade in which the worldwide sourcing of products may be as much a function of government intervention and regulation as it is of market-determined considerations of comparative cost. When foreign sourcing is driven by government intervention rather than market considerations, countries may fail to achieve the full benefits made possible by unimpeded international trade and investment.

REMEDIES

Trade-related performance requirements should be made subject to international discipline so that those demonstrably damaging to other countries' interests can be reduced or eliminated. At present, the most expeditious approach is for adversely affected countries to challenge trade-related investment policies under the GATT provisions on import quotas and export

subsidies. **New provisions specifically directed to performance requirements should be negotiated. In developing international constraints on the
use of performance requirements, allowance should be made to avoid pe-
nalizing foreign investments based on a pattern of performance requirements to which the investor was obliged to conform in the past.**

EXCHANGE RATES

As explained in Chapters 3 and 6, a country's international competitiveness can be seriously weakened if its exchange rate in relation to those
of its principal trading partners is grossly out of line with its equilibrium rate
for a sustained period of time.* This kind of situation has reached the urgent
stage in the United States today, with huge present and projected trade deficits and resultant unemployment.

Pressures are building that endanger the world trading system. Those
adversely affected perceive persistent exchange rate overvaluation as unfair. This attitude is understandable even when the misalignment is not due
to any conscious government policies to manipulate the exchange rate but
is, rather, the result of other developments at home and abroad.

The overvaluation of the dollar since 1979 has been due in part to capital inflows for safe-haven reasons (e.g., from the Middle East, Mexico,
France), but it is also in good part the consequence of high U.S. real interest
rates brought about by heavy emphasis on monetary (rather than fiscal) policy in the fight against inflation. In the case of Japan, the reverse mix of easy
monetary and tight fiscal policies has been a major factor in the undervaluation of the yen.[15] Continuing limitations on the inflow of foreign capital into
Japan and policies that enhance capital outflows also weaken the yen.

What can be done about this problem? Appropriate domestic policies
were outlined in Chapter 4, but what about international policies? *More effective international coordination of domestic macroeconomic policies is
clearly essential.* As a step toward this goal, a new study should be undertaken of the lessons to be drawn from the experience of OECD Working
Party Three, which has been attempting for years to achieve greater compat-

---

15. Japan's fiscal policy is tight compared with that of the U.S. even though both countries run budgetary
deficits equal to approximately 5 percent of GNP. The reason is that the U.S. deficit is financed out of a
pool of net private savings equal to about 6 percent of GNP, whereas Japan's net private savings are about
20 percent of GNP.

---

*See memorandum by JOHN B. CAVE, page 139.

ibility among the national economic policies of countries with different domestic objectives and priorities. [16]

The International Monetary Fund (IMF) has been assigned an important role in ensuring that countries avoid using exchange rate policy to gain unfair international competitive advantage. This function has been exercised mainly in relation to developing countries in conjunction with IMF credit operations. **We believe IMF surveillance should be strengthened in relation to the exchange rates of the industrial countries. Furthermore, we recommend that action be taken in accord with the declaration issued at the Williamsburg Summit and in conjunction with the IMF to examine means of improving the international monetary system and the possible role of an international monetary conference.**

With respect to the dollar-yen exchange rate, a closer convergence in the mix between monetary and fiscal policies in the United States and Japan is needed. In particular, tighter fiscal policies in the United States and tighter monetary policies in Japan would reduce the current misalignment by easing interest rates in the United States and raising them in Japan. In addition, the yen should be strengthened by further Japanese liberalization of capital inflows, elimination of stimuli to capital outflows, and encouragement of the international use of the yen as a reserve currency.

NATIONAL DIFFERENCES IN TAX SYSTEMS

Countries differ in the level and structure of their tax systems. These differences may affect relative costs and therefore international competitive positions. Is this a problem of unfair trade policies, and if so, what should be done about it?

GATT rules permit member countries to relieve exports of indirect domestic taxes, such as excise and value-added taxes (VAT) and to impose taxes on imports equivalent to the indirect taxes borne by comparable domestic goods. However, similar adjustments for direct taxes, such as corporate income taxes, are prohibited.

Underlying the distinction between the treatment of indirect and direct taxes is the assumption that indirect taxes are fully reflected in the price of goods but that direct taxes are fully absorbed by producers and therefore

---

16. Working Party Three carried out a two-year study of this type in the mid-1960s, i.e., when the fixed rate exchange system was still in effect. The lessons drawn from this study were set forth in "The Balance of Payments Adjustment Process," a Report by Working Party No. 3 of the Economic Policy Committee of the OECD, Paris, August 1966.

have no effect on price. Moreover, border adjustments for indirect taxes are defended on the basis of territorial taxation, i.e., such taxes are levied on transactions and should therefore be applied only by the country in which the sales transaction occurs.

It is widely believed that the distinction between the shifting of direct and indirect taxes implied in the GATT rules is weak. Some portion of direct taxes may well be shifted to consumers and some portion of indirect taxes absorbed by producers. To the extent that this is so, present border-tax-adjustment practices appear to give trade advantages to countries that rely heavily on indirect taxes, such as the members of the EEC. Exports are relieved of some taxes that are not reflected in the domestic price of goods, and imports bear some taxes that are not part of the price of domestic goods.

A counterargument is that the effects of border-tax adjustments, even if initially trade-distorting, are offset by exchange rate changes. Because an inequitable pattern of border adjustments contributes to balance-of-payments disequilibriums, it will induce an exchange rate change that compensates for the effects of the adjustments.

The type of VAT tax and the way it is administered also affect the trade advantages to countries which make border-tax adjustments for their exports. Many of the countries which rely on the border-tax adjustment on exports and imports have VAT tax systems which seem inconsistent with the rationale claimed for adjustment. To be truly consistent with the border-tax adjustment argument only the fair market value of the foreign delivery and sales activity should be *exempt* from taxation by the exporting country and subject to taxation by the importing country.

The complex questions involved in the border-tax issue have been the subject of extensive international discussion and analysis. However, no alternative to the GATT rules has been proposed that would be acceptable to a substantial number of countries. Nevertheless, the issue deserves a fresh look. **We recommend that an OECD working group be established to undertake a comprehensive study of the border-tax issue.**

In the interim, **the U.S. should continue its strong commitment to export tax benefits from either the Domestic International Sales Corporation (DISC) provisions or an equivalent replacement.** This is needed in order to put U.S. companies on a more equal footing with foreign competitors and the tax treatment of their export earnings. Export tax incentives such as DISC or an equivalent substitute are needed because they offset a variety of tax (and nontax) incentives provided by governments of our principal trading partners, help fund development of international markets and finance generally longer-term export receivables, and stimulate additional exports,

118

thereby creating more jobs for American workers.[17] Although the GATT Council adopted in 1981 a panel report to the effect that DISC violates the GATT prohibition of export subsidies, the issues noted above with respect to the GATT rules justify continuation of the current level of benefits pending completion of the comprehensive study. Therefore, **we urge that there be no reduction in the level of tax benefits currently available to exporters through DISC,** but that those benefits be provided in a manner consistent with internationally accepted principles relating to the taxation of foreign income.

SUMMARY

There is a strong trend toward an increasingly interventionist role by governments in international trade. Although the traditional modes of intervention through tariffs, formal import quotas, and explicit export subsidies may have receded, new forms of trade distortions have grown in the form of industrial policy entailing government subsidies to domestic industries, including state-owned enterprises, and the proliferation of performance requirements linked to international investment. More vigorous and expeditious enforcement of U.S. laws on unfair trade is needed to counter the adverse effects of these practices on domestic industries.

Resolving conflicts between increasing intervention by governments and the requirements of a liberal world trading system will be a major challenge for international economic diplomacy in the 1980s. Much can be accomplished through a revised GATT subsidy code including pragmatic mechanisms of consultation, conciliation, and dispute settlement. However, more explicit GATT arrangements may be needed, especially if the problems of industrial targeting, state enterprises, and performance requirements are to be dealt with effectively.

Efforts must be made to reduce major exchange rate distortions that are understandably perceived as causing unfair international competitive conditions and that therefore generate strong protectionist pressures. Questions of fairness in international trade related to differences in national tax structures should be examined.

---

17. U.S. Census Bureau estimates each $1 billion of exports supports more than 30,000 jobs.

Chapter 8

Trade in Services

Services are defined as economic activities other than mining, agriculture, fishing, and manufacturing; their distinctive feature is the intangibility of their economic output. Among the services traded internationally are such activities as accounting, advertising, auto and truck leasing, engineering, financial services, franchising, hotels, insurance, legal services, motion pictures, telecommunications, data processing and information services, and transportation.

As a group, services are of growing importance both in domestic economies and in international trade; they comprise roughly 40 percent of nongovernment gross domestic product (GDP) in most developed countries.[1] However, this figure understates the role of services because even in goods-producing industries, an increasing proportion of sales revenue comes from marketing and after-sales services. International trade in services has doubled in volume over the past decade while taking on a variety which increasingly approaches that seen in domestic service trade. No longer do services simply support traded goods (e.g., shipping and freight insurance). Some services now lead goods (e.g., information services often lead computer sales); others, such as accounting, essentially have nothing to do with goods. In short, trade in services has not only been growing rapidly but also has assumed a high degree of importance in its own right.

---

1. Committee on Invisible Exports, *Annual Report 1981/1982* (London: Committee on Invisible Exports, 1982), p. 14.

The key problem in service trade is an expanding maze of restrictions that inhibits the realization of the potential benefits of international specialization. Trade barriers in services raise local costs, discourage innovation in service activity, and artificially curtail local demand for services. In response to recession and increasing international competition, restrictions on trade in services are now accumulating virtually unchecked.

In contrast with trade in goods, no comprehensive set of international rules exists for services that would constrain arbitrary and discriminating government interventions. GATT has been devoted almost entirely to trade in goods. The OECD has two helpful multilateral codes (on the liberalization of current invisible operations and on the liberalization of capital movements), and certain sectoral conventions are sponsored by specialized United Nations agencies (e.g., the International Civil Aviation Organization and the International Maritime Consulting Organization). Typically, however, these agreements are narrowly technical and nonbinding. Sometimes they are even the source of new impediments, such as the proposed UNCTAD liner code that would reserve 40 percent of each nation's overseas trade for its own ships.

The problems created by barriers to service trade are of special significance to the United States, which has the most service-oriented economy in the world. A number of U.S. service sectors are among the most dynamic and rapidly expanding in the domestic economy. Taken as a whole, services have provided the bulk of new jobs in recent years. This rapid growth has not been at the expense of the goods-producing sector, which, though declining in relative terms, has continued to grow in absolute terms over the past two decades.[2] The United States is also the world's largest service exporter. Liberalization of trade in services is therefore a high priority for the United States. Net surpluses in U.S. service trade have contributed importantly to offsetting recent deficits in merchandise trade. As shown in Figure 8, however, the principal offset to the trade deficit is net income from foreign investment.

QUANTITATIVE IMPORTANCE OF SERVICES

THE DOMESTIC ECONOMY

Services have made up a steadily growing share of domestic economic activity (see Figure 9), reflecting rapid technological advances in transportation, communications, and data processing that have allowed many types

---

2. Ronald E. Kutscher and Jerome A. Mark, "The Service-Producing Sector: Some Common Perceptions Reviewed," *Monthly Labor Review* 10, No. 4 (April 1983): 21-24.

of services to be provided routinely and expeditiously over great distances. In response to the new opportunities, service industries have centralized, specialized, and taken advantage of economies of scale. Entirely new services have also been created, such as inventory control, computer time sharing, and cable television. The net result is that the U.S. service sector employs almost two-thirds of all nongovernment workers and provides over 60 percent of nongovernment GDP.

Not all services produced in the United States are traded internationally, however. Utility and real estate sectors, for example, provide services primarily for the domestic market and are not affected generally by foreign trade barriers.

FIGURE 8

Net U.S. Foreign Transactions

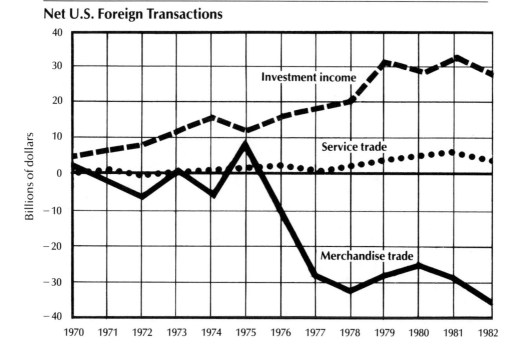

SOURCE: *The Economic Report of the President* (Washington, D.C.: U.S. Government Printing Office, February 1983). Figures for 1982 are from U.S. Department of Commerce. Both merchandise and service trade balances exclude military transactions.

FIGURE 9

Service Industry Shares of the U.S. Economy[a]

Gross domestic product

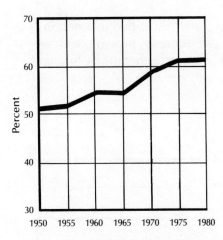

Employment

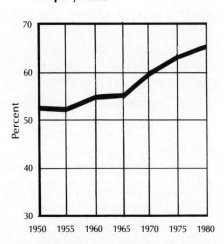

Source of wages and salary

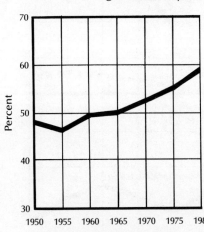

Personal consumption expenditure

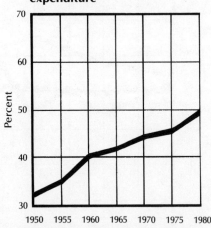

a. These data classify the service sector as including business and personal services, finance, insurance and real estate, wholesale and retail trade, and transportation and public utilities. Government activity is excluded from both the service sector and the totals for the economy.

SOURCE: *The Economic Report of the President* (February 1983); U.S. Department of Commerce, Bureau of the Census, *Statistical Abstract of the U.S.* (Washington, D.C.: U.S. Government Printing Office, 1981).

INTERNATIONAL TRADE

The same factors that underlie the growth in domestic service activities have facilitated a rapid expansion in the volume and diversity of international trade in services. However, determining just how important services have become is complicated by the absence of an internationally agreed upon definition of service trade. In the attempt to obtain quantitative assessments in this area, two problems stand out.

The first is imperfect data. Figures for the service trade are much less precise than those for trade in goods. Because most service transactions are *invisible* in the sense that they are not like products which are physically visible as they enter a country, services are thus inherently difficult to monitor, and are undoubtedly understated. Estimates are frequently resorted to, and many services are included arbitrarily in merchandise trade figures. Moreover, national accounting systems differ markedly in approaches to overcoming these difficulties. **Clearly, one of the first tasks in addressing the problems associated with trade in services is to improve and standardize the data base.** Of particular interest would be improved sectoral disaggregation and information on the job content of particular service exports and imports.

The second problem concerns the treatment of foreign investment income. Much U.S. investment income originates in the foreign affiliates of U.S. service companies in such sectors as insurance, retailing, and lodging and could be properly viewed as reflecting a service export. In fact, it probably represents the largest component of service exports because by their nature most services must be provided where they are consumed. However, investment income is not sufficiently disaggregated in officially published statistics to make clear how much originates in U.S. service activities abroad and how much is ascribable to the manufacturing and other goods-producing activities of foreign affiliates of U.S. companies. Sometimes all foreign investment income, including portfolio income, is viewed as reflecting the services of U.S. capital and therefore included in the totals for service exports. In our view, however, this concept is too broad and needlessly confuses the issue. **It would be preferable to include in service exports only that portion of foreign investment income originating in service activities abroad.**

Service exports can be broken down into the following four categories: produced and sold at home to nonresidents (tourism, education, medical care), produced at home and sold abroad (advertising, motion pictures, publishing), produced and sold abroad (retailing, insurance, hospital management), and provided in global commons to nonresidents (shipping, travel, satellite communications). The foreign revenues of the U.S. service sector in 1980 for these four categories is estimated at $60 billion.[3] Total distribution is shown in Figure 10.

Service trade has made an important contribution to offsetting recent deficits in the U.S. merchandise trade. Unfortunately, the extent of that contribution cannot be defined precisely because income from service activities abroad is not regularly disaggregated. Figures comparable to those given for 1980 are not available for other years or for service imports in any year. Nevertheless, some indication of the net contribution of services to the U.S. balance of payments can be ascertained from Figure 8. Even defined narrowly to exclude investment income from U.S. service activities overseas, exports of services earn the United States about $7 billion annually over and above the cost of imported services.

IMPEDIMENTS TO TRADE

REASONS FOR RESTRICTIONS

Some restrictions are outright protectionist measures intended to shield domestic service activities from external competition. Others reflect government policies not directly related to trade protection.

Many service sectors have been subject to extensive government regulation. Even *within* the United States, there are continuing restrictions on certain interstate service trade that stand in contrast with the free interstate trade in goods dating back to the founding of the Republic. Although some service sectors, such as shipping and communications, are moving toward deregulation, restrictions remain, for example, on interstate banking, and the individual states license lawyers, doctors, and engineers practicing within their jurisdictions. Given the absence of free trade in services even among states, it is not surprising that restrictions among nations would be more severe. That this is the case is shown in the 230-page list of restrictions (admittedly incomplete) faced by U.S. service exporters compiled by the Office of the U.S. Trade Representative in 1982.

Four main motives underlie many of the restrictions on trade in services.

PROTECTION OF THE PUBLIC INTEREST. Some regulation of service activity is justified to protect the public interest (e.g., in insurance, fiduciary interest; in data processing, confidentiality). Meeting this public

---

3. Economic Consulting Services Inc., "The International Operations of U.S. Service Industries: Current Data Collection and Analysis," (Washington, D.C.: Commissioned by the Office of the U.S. Trade Representative, mimeographed, June 1981).

FIGURE 10

Total Distribution
Foreign Revenues of the U.S. Service Sector, 1980[a]

Service Industry	Foreign Revenues (billions)
Accounting	$2.35
Advertising	2.05
Banking[b]	9.10
Business and professional technical service	1.07
Construction and engineering	5.36
Education	1.27
Employment	0.55
Franchising	1.26
Health	0.27
Information	0.60
Insurance	6.00
Leasing	2.35
Lodging	4.60
Motion pictures	1.14
Tourism	4.15
Transportation	13.95
Total for 16 service industries	56.06
Miscellaneous financial services, communications, and so on	4.00 (est.)
Total U.S. service sector	60.00

a. Service exports in this figure represent the four categories listed on page 123.

b. Includes $7.4 billion in net interest income.

SOURCE: See Footnote 3.

126

trust is perceived as more difficult when the service activity is carried on by foreign firms (e.g., if confidential data are stored abroad).

EXERCISE OF CONTROL. Government often intervenes in services in order to have a greater degree of centralized political and economic control (e.g., through state enterprises in broadcasting and banking). Restrictions are imposed on banks and insurance companies (especially life insurance) because of their role as financial intermediaries and on banks as sources of credit. Most countries have justified such restrictions in terms of the need to control savings and investments. With domestic competition effectively limited, it is understandable that governments do not open these fields freely to foreigners.

TECHNOLOGICAL INDEPENDENCE. Many countries, especially those in the Third World, are wary of becoming excessively and perhaps irreversibly dependent on foreign nations for services involving critical skills such as engineering, information processing, or financial management. Restrictions on foreign activities in these fields bear a resemblance to infant-industry protection in the goods trade. Establishing an indigenous technological capacity is often regarded as even more fundamental to true development than the success of one or another goods-producing industry.

CULTURAL AND SOCIAL VALUES. Many countries impose restrictions on foreign-supplied services such as advertising, communications, and education as a means of preserving, disseminating, and encouraging national, cultural, and social values.

FORMS OF RESTRICTIONS

Restrictions on services fall into two broad categories: trade-related and investment-related.

Trade-related distortions to trade in services are similar to nontariff impediments to trade in goods. Examples are quantitative restrictions, outright exclusion, discriminatory standards, favoritism in government procurement, and subsidies and other forms of assistance to domestic competitors.

Investment-related distortions mainly affect services produced abroad by affiliates of U.S. firms. As is true for direct foreign investment generally, such activities are subject to many forms of discriminatory and restrictive practices. Examples are limitations on the right of establishment and deviations from national treatment, including performance requirements, bureaucratic delays, differential taxes and regulatory enforcement, local-content, or local-ownership requirements, discrimination by government-owned suppliers such as utilities, and restrictions on access to domestic telecommunication networks.

Many national laws (e.g., visa and immigration restrictions, employment laws and regulations, foreign exchange controls, and restrictions on the import of accessory goods and services, repatriation of profits, and transborder data flows) may not explicitly deviate from national treatment but in practice constitute a special burden on foreign firms.

ISSUES IN NEGOTIATING THE REDUCTION OF IMPEDIMENTS

GENERAL RULES VERSUS SECTORAL AGREEMENTS

Because of the diversity of service industries, a program may have to be designed to achieve the actual reduction or elimination of barriers aimed specifically at individual service sectors. However, it would be much more desirable if an agreement on services could be fashioned by incorporating several principles normally included in trade and investment agreements. Specific problems are associated with each dimension of such a package.

TRADE ISSUES. Tariffs are unimportant in service trade,[4] but there are many nontariff barriers. **The objective should be to identify and reduce these barriers and guard against new ones.**

- As a first step, transparency should be required so that barriers to trade in services can be clearly identified.

- A detailed study should be undertaken to determine the most effective techniques to reduce barriers.

- Securing most-favored-nation (MFN) treatment,[5] as a minimum, should be possible for all existing barriers.

INVESTMENT ISSUES. Because virtually all countries limit the right of foreigners to own affiliates in certain sensitive service sectors, exceptions to national treatment with respect to establishment or acquisition will have to be provided for. **However, such exceptions should be minimized and made explicit and should be subject to the MFN principle. Once foreign firms are established, both MFN and national-treatment principles should apply.**

INTERNATIONAL NEGOTIATION AND GOVERNMENT REGULATION

The more extensive domestic government regulations, the greater the opportunities there are in the actual application of the regulations for dis-

---

4. In transborder data flows, however, countries may assess a tax on each bit of information as it crosses the border.

---

5. Most-favored-nation treatment is the best trade privilege granted to another nation.

crimination against foreign providers of services. Safeguards should be developed in the form of facilities for dispute settlement, including arbitration.

Another negotiating problem is the division of domestic regulatory authority subnationally or among bureaucratic agencies. In the United States, for example, insurance is regulated at the state level, and much of banking is regulated by authorities at both the state and the federal levels. **In cases of multiple jurisdictions, regulatory authorities, particularly at the state level, should take greater account of the effects of their policies and practices on reciprocal access for American service companies to foreign markets.**

TRADE-OFFS

It is unlikely that other countries will make concessions if the United States does not. In negotiating the liberalization of service trade, the United States will have to think in terms of the reciprocal actions that may be demanded by others. Some may prove to be extremely difficult to accept, for example, giving Third World workers access to the U.S. construction industry in return for access to Third World markets for U.S. technical professionals.

U.S. barriers to foreign participation do exist in some service sectors (e.g., wireless communication facilities, shipping, and aviation). Even though these restrictions reflect both political sensitivities and powerful domestic constituencies, they may have to be included in any comprehensive negotiation.

Nevertheless, the United States probably imposes fewer restrictions on services trade than other nations, and recent deregulation has reduced these restrictions even further. To the extent that the relative openness of the U.S. market to foreign service activity deprives the United States of bargaining power, it could prove a problem in future negotiations.

POSITION OF THE DEVELOPING COUNTRIES

There are great differences in the importance of service trade and individual service categories to different regions and countries in the developing world. Tourism is especially important for southern Europe, some Latin American countries, and a few nations in Asia and Africa. Because of the common practice of registering ships under flags of convenience, the commercial fleets of Panama and Liberia have been growing rapidly. A more recent development is the large volume of construction services exported by some newly industrialized countries, notably South Korea, Taiwan, and Yugoslavia.

Despite large exports of particular categories of services, the developing countries are, with few exceptions, in substantial deficit on overall service account.[6] In order to conserve foreign exchange and encourage the development of indigenous service industries, they have resorted to a wide variety of trade and investment restrictions. Under present circumstances, therefore, little interest can be expected on the part of developing countries in worldwide negotiations based on reciprocity or market access and including obligations with respect to the treatment of foreign investment.

Of course, the attitude of the developing countries toward negotiating might change if they were offered parallel liberalization of merchandise trade in return for concessions on services. Moreover, as in the case of trade in goods, they would undoubtedly demand special and differential treatment entailing suspension of the reciprocity obligation at least for a limited period.

From a long-term perspective, it would generally be in the best interest of developing countries to participate in negotiations on trade in services. **Participation would provide them with an opportunity to influence the shape of the new rules and to acquire rights to liberalized treatment for their own service exports, which may assume greater importance in the not too distant future as comparative advantage changes.**

PROSPECTS FOR INTERNATIONAL NEGOTIATIONS ON SERVICES

The United States has been the most aggressive nation in promoting liberalization of service trade, sponsoring a major initiative at the GATT ministerial meeting in November 1982. However, there was little enthusiasm for the U.S. initiative even among the industrial countries. For a number of reasons, including a lack of prior study of the matter, preoccupation with other trade issues, skepticism about the possibilities of success, and especially, the feeling that it was the United States that had the most to gain, few industrial countries shared this enthusiasm. Moreover, many services issues are really investment issues; and according to some countries, these should not be dealt with in the context of GATT.

The indifference among the European countries that characterized the discussion of services at the ministerial meeting has now been largely dissipated. After long hesitation, the EEC has decided to back multilateral efforts to bolster world trade in services. The move resulted from recent internal

---

6. Andre Sapir and Ernest Lutz, "Trade in Non-Factor Services: Past Trends and Current Issues," World Bank Staff Working Paper no. 410, August 1980.

130

studies that showed that a third of the EEC's total trade involves service industries. As a consequence of this shift in position, there is now a broad consensus among industrial countries that negotiation of an international discipline for trade in services is essential.

A PROGRAM OF ACTION

STEPS THE UNITED STATES CAN TAKE

One step that this nation can take unilaterally to improve the prospects for its service trade is to **review its own policies and revise those that may discourage or discriminate against service exports** (e.g., those pertaining to foreign corrupt practices, the taxation of personal income earned abroad, and eligibility for Export-Import Bank financing deserve special consideration).

U.S. service exporters should be aware of deep-seated foreign concerns about preserving national autonomy in sensitive service sectors. Where countries discriminate against foreign firms in such fields as banking, insurance, and data processing, U.S. firms should seriously consider establishing joint ventures with local companies as a way of minimizing concerns.

The United States responded quickly to the GATT ministerial call for national examination of service issues. A thorough report was submitted at the December 1983 GATT meeting. **Negotiation would be helped not only by the comprehensive inventory of restrictions the United States faces abroad, which is included in the study, but also by the addition of an inventory of U.S. barriers faced by foreign nations.**

INTERIM INTERNATIONAL ACTION

A binding and comprehensive agreement is clearly beyond reach in the immediate future. **The interim aim, therefore, should be to establish an international body without rule-making authority, preferably within GATT. It would be composed of the largest number of countries that can be attracted to take part.**

The new body should establish a broad set of guiding principles, meet at regular intervals to exchange information, provide a forum for consultations, and facilitate the settlement of disputes. It might also attempt to achieve a standstill with respect to new impediments to trade in services. At the very least, this would legitimize services as a trade issue and provide a framework within which specific rules for trade in services could be negotiated.

INTERNATIONAL AGREEMENTS

The United States should encourage early talks within GATT leading to the negotiation of a liberal trading regime for services. The aim of negotiations should be to reduce barriers to trade and investment in services and to establish a set of common rules to govern this sector of international commerce. Barriers should be made public, explicit, and subject to negotiation. Internal government regulations should be applied on a national-treatment basis. The right to purchase from and sell to government monopolies should be available to foreign firms on the same terms provided to private domestic companies.

Because of the inherent difficulties, the most effective means of negotiating would be an approach on several levels, both horizontally (to include more countries) and vertically (to include more sectors).

BILATERAL COUNTRY COVERAGE. **By tailoring each agreement to meet the problems of specific negotiating partners, otherwise-reluctant nations can be brought more effectively into the negotiating process.** However, care should be taken that this approach is not pursued in a way (e.g., exclusivity clauses) that would conflict with multilateral objectives.

MULTILATERAL COUNTRY COVERAGE. **Multilateral negotiations might begin among like-minded members of the OECD.** Not all OECD countries are equally interested in such an initiative, but background work has begun there, and most members agree at least on the general desirability of liberalization. **Ultimately, an agreement initiated within the OECD could be absorbed at the GATT level and could be expanded to include those developing countries prepared to participate.** In certain instances, existing GATT articles and codes may be interpreted or expanded to include services.

SECTORAL COVERAGE. **It is unlikely that any bilateral or multilateral agreement would apply initially to all service sectors. Within a broad set of guiding principles for trade in services, however, a start should be made to negotiate more specific rules for those sectors where agreement is feasible.** Precedents exist in air travel and some types of communication. Multisectoral agreements should be pursued whenever possible.

SUMMARY

Service industries are a rapidly expanding sector of the U.S. economy. They also play an important role in offsetting large U.S. deficits in merchandise trade. Beyond any special U.S. interests, however, expanding opportunities for trade in services should be sought because such trade brings all participants many of the same benefits derived from liberalized trade in goods.

The growing complex of restrictions and the virtual absence of effective rules applying to trade in services make it imperative to begin a process of reducing restrictions and establishing a stable institutional environment for this sector of international trade. Now that the EEC recognizes a common interest in this field, it should be invited to join the United States in taking the lead.

The guiding principles in service trade negotiations should be openness of regulations and restrictions, reciprocal negotiability of reductions in barriers, nondiscrimination and national treatment with respect to internal regulation, and the early establishment of effective data collection, consultation, and dispute-settlement facilities.

The United States should be flexible in its approach to service negotiations. Although the ultimate objective is a universal and wide-ranging agreement — in effect, a GATT for services — this country should be prepared to begin on a more modest basis with respect to the content of the agreement and its geographic and sectoral coverage.

Memoranda of Comment, Reservation, or Dissent

Page 2, by HENRY B. SCHACHT, with which FLETCHER L. BYROM and JOHN DIEBOLD have asked to be associated

These perhaps seemingly positive statistics and projections by themselves should offer little comfort. Absent the adoption of this study's major policy recommendations for aligning exchange rates, reducing the deficit, and enhancing productivity and international competitiveness through a broad range of policy changes, the statistics and projections about manufacturing and employment cited here are likely in retrospect to have been unrealistically optimistic. If policy changes along these lines are not soon put into effect, U.S. manufacturing strength and employment may well deteriorate rapidly (and perhaps irreversibly) despite essential efforts by management and labor to improve competitiveness at the firm level. There is, as the study states on p. 6, an urgent need for immediate action on CED's recommendations to improve the competitiveness of both manufacturing and nonmanufacturing industries.

Page 7, by JOHN DIEBOLD

While I strongly agree that reliance on the market system is the best way to spur growth and insure competitiveness, we must also recognize that government already exerts tremendous influence on the economy, and that its monetary, fiscal, tax and regulatory decisions constitute an elaborate, if *de facto*, "industrial policy." It seems to me we should not only recognize this, but regularly review it to insure that these decisions are consistent and not stifling to the economy.

So far, the record from Administration to Administration has been disappointing. Each chooses some mechanism for final review and clearance of economic policy, but in reality the choices get made by the political staff, or by lower-level bureaucrats whose interests conflict with each other. In the current Administration, for example, there is an Office of Policy Development, whose mandate is to oversee policymaking so that initiatives all move in the same direction. But it is seen as a relatively weak influence. Power actually resides with the top White House staff, or with the heads of certain key administrative departments.

The decision in February 1981 to route all new regulatory initiatives through a final OMB review was a wise one, and a similar mechanism should be adopted on a broader scale to insure that all new policy initiatives reflect true long-range national interests. The Office of Policy Development could be the locus of such a function, but it would have to be guaranteed a stronger voice in final policy deliberations — perhaps through some administrative integration with the highest levels of White House staff.

Added government intervention in private markets will accomplish nothing, and may do a great deal of harm. But there is no reason why a more coherent and rationally organized Executive need be feared, and I view it as the key to improving economic policy overall.

Page 10, by HENRY B. SCHACHT, with which FLETCHER L. BYROM and ELMER B. STAATS have asked to be associated

Necessary to the success of the three main areas of government policy change recommended by this study is a neutral, competent, *central* source of information and analysis within the federal government on U.S. competitiveness and foreign competition. Combined with information on innovation and competitive policies in each major country as recommended by CED on p. 112, this capacity could provide early warning for U.S. policy makers and interested parties and the means for assessing the impact of proposed U.S. and foreign governmental actions on U.S. international competitiveness by industry sector and in the aggregate. Some of this is already available in various U.S. agencies but in a fragmented fashion (and it is done more effectively by U.S. competitors such as the U.K. and Japan). Improving and centralizing (perhaps in the Department of Commerce) the collection, analysis, and dissemination of this information would enhance the working of market forces and significantly increase the potential for strengthening U.S. international competitiveness.

136

Page 10, by ELMER B. STAATS, with which FLETCHER L. BYROM and JOHN DIEBOLD have asked to be associated

One difficulty in achieving a national policy to increase industrial competitiveness and productivity has been the absence of a central point in government which has responsibility for advising on the total range of issues included in the CED report. The Reagan Administration is to be commended for establishing the Commission on Industrial Competitiveness which has yet to report. This Commission, however, is temporary and its report, however useful, will need continuing, high-level, and visible attention and discussion among labor, business, and government if it is to be effective.

The CED report *Productivity Policy: Key to the Nation's Economic Future* suggested the need for such a point in government to accomplish this objective. That recommendation needs reiteration with the issuance of this report. Without such a focal point in government I believe the chances for achieving many of the recommendations of the CED reports will be greatly lessened.

Page 13, by JAMES Q. RIORDAN

The report is excellent. It reaffirms in a comprehensive and integrated manner policy positions that CED has espoused over the years, i.e., greater reliance on free market forces and support for economic policies that encourage adjustment and innovation. We need to be able to compete effectively in the world market governed by generally comparable rules. The report properly highlights the need to improve our tax system to make it simpler and more neutral; lower marginal rates; simplify the tax base; and eliminate disincentives to invest and innovate. In these circumstances I think it would have been better for us to grasp the nettle and recommend that the United States should help itself by accommodating to world practice and adopting the value added tax system. This would eliminate the need to call for an OECD working group to undertake still another study of the border tax issue and would put in place a revenue source for the U.S. government that will be required in any event if there is to be any realistic hope of achieving the other improvements in our tax structure that are recommended throughout the report. Congress is not likely to accept the revenue loss involved in our tax recommendations (e.g., the immediate deductability of business investment) unless the loss can be recouped from a new revenue source (e.g., the value added tax). I think we have missed an opportunity to state clearly that we favor solving the border tax issue by doing what we ought to do in any event.

Page 18, by JACK F. BENNETT, with which EMILIO G. COLLADO has asked to be associated

In the market place I see no justification for statements in this report that the U.S. dollar is overvalued and that real interest rates are higher in the United States. Of course, the excessive borrowing by the U.S. government bodies does raise the world level of real interest rates and does raise the foreign exchange value of the dollar. Under the circumstances, I do not see any value in the U.S. government borrowing more in order — as this report seems to favor — to invest in a portfolio of foreign currency receivables. Nor would it be wise to follow the report's advice to coordinate U.S. financial policies with those of the other OECD governments. We should do better. On average the others have been borrowing an even larger percentage of GNP than has the United States.

I see no objection to the recommendation that Japan remove restrictions on its capital markets even though I suspect the result in the near future, if any, is as likely to be a lowering of the dollar value of the yen as a raising of its value.

Page 21, by THEODORE A. BURTIS, with which W. BRUCE THOMAS has asked to be associated

Although employee compensation differentials are major determinants of an industry's competitiveness, capital cost differentials are also important. Recent studies have shown that the high cost of equity capital may retard investment in America's basic industries and thereby reduce their ability to compete internationally. A hybrid equity issue with tax advantages would lower the cost. A tax-favored preferred equity would permit efficient capital allocation without direct Federal support. It would lower the cost of equity by partially eliminating the double taxation of dividends.

Page 26, by J. W. McSWINEY

An important advantage of expanding international trade is the redistribution of production activities to take advantage of the low-cost labor supply in developing nations. This permits developing countries to raise their standard of living through greater participation in world economic activities, which is in the long-run interest of the United States and the rest of the free world. At the same time, however, the gradual process of relocation of production facilities must take place in an environment of expanding international trade in which U.S. companies can take advantage of industrial restructuring by shifting resources to high-skilled production activities. If U.S. companies fail to adjust to this process of change through productivity improvement and compensation flexibility there could be an unnecessary loss of jobs to foreign sourcing. Yet, the risk to U.S. firms that elect to retain their domestic production facilities is substantially greater than to those that elect to transfer offshore. This will require, in some cases, some form of temporary government protection to enable such firms to make those innovations necessary to compete. Although there is a risk that some firms may come to rely upon such assistance, the risk can be greatly mitigated if the assistance is strictly limited in duration and accompanied by strong conditions on performance.

Page 27, by CLIFTON R. WHARTON, JR.

Presumably the issue here is government's first *economic* responsibility, since most citizens would assume the responsibilities for keeping domestic order and ensuring national security to be paramount. Even with that proviso, however, the generalization is open to question; it might be argued with considerable force that government's first economic duties are collecting taxes and expending them on useful and necessary public works and facilities.

What is stated as fact is actually a clearly ideological view of the relationship between government and the market. The conventional corporate view is that government activity outside the narrow bounds prescribed is seen as a departure from desired norms, e.g., the argument that "industrial policy" will inevitably entail "increased government intervention." Yet many advocates of industrial policy (particularly Lester Thurow) cogently insist that such policies aim less at fostering new public-private sector interdependencies than at organizing and rationalizing existing ones for greater effect.

Pages 38 and 115, by JOHN B. CAVE

Whereas exchange rate equilibrium among trading partners is always to be desired and should be an objective of trading partners, my experience and recollection is that some disequilibrium often exists. This situation will probably continue as long as we can project in the future. The policy statement implies that the present over-valued status of the U.S. dollar is perhaps unique and it provides only passing reference to the fact that the U.S. dollar has in several cases in the past been substantially under-valued. During those under-valued periods I do not recall a strong protest from U.S. business or a comment in prior CED policy statements that this disequilibrium should be corrected. In my judgment the policy statement is not properly balanced on this particular issue.

Page 42, by FRAZAR B. WILDE

While this policy statement is a good illustration of how we wish our economy would work it fails to recognize the urgent need for government action to ensure an abundant, reasonably priced, and secure source of power for U.S. industry. This could be done by authorizing a reconstruction finance corporation, which served us well in the past. Over the years government policy toward nuclear power has been short-sighted and ineffective as illustrated by the failure to implement the Seabrook Project as a reliable source of power without incurring excessive costs. This has been harmful to economic development in New England in general and especially in Connecticut. As a result we have been forced to rely on the willingness of our neighboring country Canada to sell us hydroelectric power. The U.S. government has a responsibility for ensuring that our country is in the long run self-sufficient in its needs for the power necessary for a strong economy. The experience of rescuing New York City, which was led by Felix Rohatyn of Lazard Freres, is a good illustration of how the right leadership from the private sector and government might produce a successful and constructive energy program.

Page 44, by EDMUND B. FITZGERALD, with which JOHN DIEBOLD has asked to be associated

While I am in agreement with the intent of these guidelines, I would like to emphasize that the policies adopted to achieve them must be carefully crafted to avoid "policy-induced uncertainty." Some of our trading partners have very skillfully used the perception of inconsistency in past U.S. policy on high-tech exports to discourage potential foreign customers from doing business with us because of our alleged inability to guarantee long-term product support.

Similarly, "policy-induced uncertainty" creates delays in the approval process, which deter effective marketing and sales efforts and often cause the mis-application of valuable technology, marketing and sales resources to opportunities to which we are ultimately denied access.

Finally, high-tech exports must be intelligently analyzed in light of the availability of similar products from other nations who do not practice the same technology export restraint as does the United States. If equivalent alternatives already exist in the East or are available from other nations, denial of U.S. export license does significant harm to the attainment of our current and future global market shares in product areas vital to achieving our goal of enhanced industrial competitiveness.

Page 44, by FRANKLIN A. LINDSAY, with which FLETCHER L. BYROM has asked to be associated

The current system of national security controls on exports is not effective in keeping the list of products and processes under such control up to date. It makes no sense to continue controls on technologies once they are no longer critically significant or when the technology is readily available from uncontrolled sources outside the United States. Part of the problem with the present system is that controls are seldom removed. U.S. export policy should provide a stronger motivation toward maintaining an up-to-date list of controlled goods and technologies. One approach would be to automatically remove each technology or product from the export control list after four years unless the government presents evidence that the specific control is still essential to national security. This type of sunset provision is especially relevant for controls on exports imposed unilaterally by the U.S. government. In the case of controls agreed upon with our allies, the U.S. government should take the initiative in reevaluating existing controls every four years.

Page 46, by PHILIP M. KLUTZNICK, with which ELMER B. STAATS has asked to be associated

The general tenor of the statement's views on competitive strategy could be interpreted to exclude appropriate roles for the government in industrial activity. The words "industrial policy" are subject to many connotations. Our government is today actively engaged in a variety of ways in what one might consider involvement in "industrial policy."

For example, the federal government gathers and supplies information on a regular basis on the status of our economy as well as on the status of various sectors of our economy. It also engages in a variety of interventions that affect industrial and commercial activities.

Without creating new or massive machinery, it should be possible for the government to assist the normal market processes by utilizing what it has at hand.

It could create a system of sectoral groups consisting of industry, labor and government which attempts to utilize the massive information available sector-by-sector to ascertain in advance where possible whether or not there are areas that are in need of special attention by the marketplace or the government itself.

It is not only the private sector that makes a difference in competitiveness. It may be as the statement points out, that outmoded regulations, antitrust or banking laws or other areas in which the government intervenes need attention and correction. We should be able by proper collaboration to anticipate and correct practices which reduce our competitiveness.

I would assume that this statement in its emphasis on the reliance to a greater degree on the market system, does not exclude strengthening the appropriate government role which does not interfere with the market system, but could well strengthen it.

Page 54, by CLIFTON R. WHARTON, JR., with which FLETCHER L. BYROM has asked to be associated

I offer the following comment at the risk of appearing parochial, and with acknowledgment that past and future CED policy statements may address my concerns more adequately than would be possible in the present document.

142

Nevertheless, I am obliged to note that while the report mentions the importance of basic education for a productive and adaptable workforce, the report fails to discuss the centrality of higher education in national economic development. Not only does higher education prepare its graduates for technically specialized jobs and positions in civic, business, scientific, and cultural leadership, it is also a primary locus of innovation, research, and development. Many of the most exciting of today's new technologies (e.g., computerization and artificial intelligence, biotechnology) emerged from college and university laboratories and there is every reason to believe that many of tomorrow's key discoveries will take place in the same setting.

It is crucial, therefore, that the increasingly intimate ties between business and higher education be built on an explicit recognition of the integral role campus-based teaching and research must continue to play in our nation's industrial revitalization. This point was emphasized in the recently issued report of the Business-Higher Education Forum.

Page 66, by THEODORE A. BURTIS, with which W. BRUCE THOMAS has asked to be associated

The efficiency of the UI system can also be improved by taking into account employer severance benefits for the purposes of unemployment compensation. The wide variation in severance arrangements warrants tying these payments to unemployment payments to produce permanent UI savings by eliminating redundancy.

Page 80, by W. BRUCE THOMAS, with which FLETCHER L. BYROM has asked to be associated

U.S. firms can bring complaints against foreign companies under U.S. trade laws and thereby limit the effects of foreign competition. This has been a concern for antitrust authorities. Market definitions for antitrust purposes need to be harmonized with international competitive realities, recognizing that even with the elimination of unfair trade practices by foreign companies (injurious price discrimination and below-cost selling), competition would remain vigorous enough to preserve the United States as an international market. Foreign competitors adhering to U.S. trade laws would participate on an equal basis with domestic companies and should be counted as full market participants for antitrust purposes.

144

OBJECTIVES OF THE COMMITTEE FOR ECONOMIC DEVELOPMENT

For over forty years, the Committee for Economic Development has been a respected influence on the formation of business and public policy. CED is devoted to these two objectives:

To develop, through objective research and informed discussion, findings and recommendations for private and public policy that will contribute to preserving and strengthening our free society, achieving steady economic growth at high employment and reasonably stable prices, increasing productivity and living standards, providing greater and more equal opportunity for every citizen, and improving the quality of life for all.

To bring about increasing understanding by present and future leaders in business, government, and education, and among concerned citizens, of the importance of these objectives and the ways in which they can be achieved.

CED's work is supported strictly by private voluntary contributions from business and industry, foundations, and individuals. It is independent, nonprofit, nonpartisan, and nonpolitical.

The two hundred trustees, who generally are presidents or board chairmen of corporations and presidents of universities, are chosen for their individual capacities rather than as representatives of any particular interests. By working with scholars, they unite business judgment and experience with scholarship in analyzing the issues and developing recommendations to resolve the economic problems that constantly arise in a dynamic and democratic society.

Through this business-academic partnership, CED endeavors to develop policy statements and other research materials that commend themselves as guides to public and business policy; that can be used as texts in college economics and political science courses and in management training courses; that will be considered and discussed by newspaper and magazine editors, columnists, and commentators; and that are distributed abroad to promote better understanding of the American economic system.

CED believes that by enabling businessmen to demonstrate constructively their concern for the general welfare, it is helping business to earn and maintain the national and community respect essential to the successful functioning of the free enterprise capitalist system.

HONORARY TRUSTEES

STATEMENTS ON NATIONAL POLICY
ISSUED BY THE RESEARCH AND POLICY COMMITTEE

SELECTED PUBLICATIONS

Strategy for U.S. Industrial Competitiveness *(April 1984)*

Strengthening the Federal Budget Process:
  A Requirement for Effective Fiscal Control *(June 1983)*

Productivity Policy: Key to the Nation's Economic Future *(April 1983)*

Energy Prices and Public Policy *(July 1982)*

Public-Private Partnership: An Opportunity for Urban Communities
  (February 1982)

Reforming Retirement Policies *(September 1981)*

Transnational Corporations and Developing Countries: New Policies for a
  Changing World Economy *(April 1981)*

Fighting Inflation and Rebuilding a Sound Economy *(September 1980)*

Stimulating Technological Progress *(January 1980)*

Helping Insure Our Energy Future:
  A Program for Developing Synthetic Fuel Plants Now *(July 1979)*

Redefining Government's Role in the Market System *(July 1979)*

Improving Management of the Public Work Force:
  The Challenge to State and Local Government *(November 1978)*

Jobs for the Hard-to-Employ:
  New Directions for a Public-Private Partnership *(January 1978)*

An Approach to Federal Urban Policy *(December 1977)*

Key Elements of a National Energy Strategy *(June 1977)*

The Economy in 1977–78: Strategy for an Enduring Expansion *(December 1976)*

Nuclear Energy and National Security *(September 1976)*

Fighting Inflation and Promoting Growth *(August 1976)*

Improving Productivity in State and Local Government *(March 1976)*

*International Economic Consequences of High-Priced Energy *(September 1975)*

Broadcasting and Cable Television:
  Policies for Diversity and Change *(April 1975)*

Achieving Energy Independence *(December 1974)*

A New U.S. Farm Policy for Changing World Food Needs *(October 1974)*

Congressional Decision Making for National Security *(September 1974)*

*Toward a New International Economic System:
  A Joint Japanese-American View *(June 1974)*

More Effective Programs for a Cleaner Environment *(April 1974)*

The Management and Financing of Colleges *(October 1973)*

Strengthening the World Monetary System *(July 1973)*

Financing the Nation's Housing Needs *(April 1973)*

Building a National Health-Care System *(April 1973)*

*A New Trade Policy Toward Communist Countries *(September 1972)*

High Employment Without Inflation:
   A Positive Program for Economic Stabilization *(July 1972)*

Reducing Crime and Assuring Justice *(June 1972)*

Military Manpower and National Security *(February 1972)*

The United States and the European Community:
   Policies for a Changing World Economy *(November 1971)*

Improving Federal Program Performance *(September 1971)*

Social Responsibilities of Business Corporations *(June 1971)*

Education for the Urban Disadvantaged:
   From Preschool to Employment *(March 1971)*

Further Weapons Against Inflation *(November 1970)*

Making Congress More Effective *(September 1970)*

Training and Jobs for the Urban Poor *(July 1970)*

Improving the Public Welfare System *(April 1970)*

Reshaping Government in Metropolitan Areas *(February 1970)*

Economic Growth in the United States *(October 1969)*

Assisting Development in Low-Income Countries *(September 1969)*

*Nontariff Distortions of Trade *(September 1969)*

Fiscal and Monetary Policies for Steady Economic Growth *(January 1969)*

Financing a Better Election System *(December 1968)*

Innovation in Education: New Directions for the American School *(July 1968)*

Modernizing State Government *(July 1967)*

*Trade Policy Toward Low-Income Countries *(June 1967)*

How Low Income Countries Can Advance Their Own Growth *(September 1966)*

Modernizing Local Government *(July 1966)*

Budgeting for National Objectives *(January 1966)*

*Statements issued in association with CED counterpart organizations in foreign countries.

CED COUNTERPART ORGANIZATIONS IN FOREIGN COUNTRIES

Close relations exist between the Committee for Economic Development and independent, nonpolitical research organizations in other countries. Such counterpart groups are composed of business executives and scholars and have objectives similar to those of CED, which they pursue by similarly objective methods. CED cooperates with these organizations on research and study projects of common interest to the various countries concerned. This program has resulted in a number of joint policy statements involving such international matters as energy, East-West trade, assistance to the developing countries, and the reduction of nontariff barriers to trade.

CE	Círculo de Empresarios Serrano Jover 5-2°, Madrid 8, Spain
CEDA	Committee for Economic Development of Australia 139 Macquarie Street, Sydney 2001, New South Wales, Australia
CEPES	Europäische Vereinigung für Wirtschaftliche und Soziale Entwicklung Reuterweg 14,6000 Frankfurt/Main, West Germany
IDEP	Institut de l'Entreprise 6, rue Clément-Marot, 75008 Paris, France
経済同友会	Keizai Doyukai (Japan Committee for Economic Development) Japan Industrial Club Bldg. 1 Marunouchi, Chiyoda-ku, Tokyo, Japan
PSI	Policy Studies Institute 1-2 Castle Lane, London SW1E 6DR, England
SNS	Studieförbundet Näringsliv och Samhälle Sköldungagatan 2, 11427 Stockholm, Sweden

DATE DUE

DEMCO 38-297